LETTERS FROM

AN

ACCIDENTAL

OPTIMIST

LETTERS FROM

AN

ACCIDENTAL

OPTIMIST

Pandemic Notes on
Life, Leadership, and
Lifting Each Other Up

SAMRAT SHENBAGA

CLEARSIGHT
BOOKS

Raleigh, North Carolina

ISBN hardback: 978-1-945209-23-9
ISBN ebook: 978-1-945209-24-6
Library of Congress Control Number: 2021923584
Published by Clear Sight Books, Raleigh, North Carolina
Book and Cover Design by Patricia Saxton

To my father, who encouraged me to dream, and my mother, who pushed me to turn those dreams into reality.

To my Compellium team, whose dedication, compassion, and humility inspire me every day and make me realize how fortunate I am.

And finally, in memory of my good friends Cutie the cat and Riley the dog. Cutie kept me company during the writing process and provided amusement with his varied reactions to my work. Riley's big heart and free spirit always put a smile on my face and made me a better man. You can find the most precious Rileyisms at the end of this book.

DISCLAIMER

This book was accomplished by me in my personal capacity. The views, information, and opinions expressed in this book are my own and do not reflect the views of any entity with which I have been, am now, or will be affiliated.

CONTENTS

INTRODUCTION

Friday, April 16, 2021

To: Compellium Team
From: Samrat Shenbaga
Subject: PRODUCTIVE UTILIZATION
OF ONESELF DURING A PANDEMIC

Compellium Team:

It was great to see many of you during the town hall yesterday. The energy and enthusiasm you bring to everything every day continues to fill me with great Pride and Joy for being part of this team. With the virus on the rise in India, our colleagues there are once again facing the stress of lockdowns, morbid projections, and (for a few) the physical effects of the virus. It is a tough time and it got me reflecting back to pre-Thanksgiving when the US surge was in full swing. The prospect of being stuck at home for the entire holiday season, flipping between a constantly bewildered Anderson Cooper and an eternally constipated-looking Tucker Carlson while excessively imbibing Scotch, gave me the chills. Just then, in response to one of my emails, a team member wrote, "If you ever write a book, I would read it." Voilà—there it was (note: he said "read" not "buy").

For some time I have pondered what my response will be 15 years from now when someone asks what I did during my professional career. "Partner at a management consulting firm" is such a boring answer. But "I wrote a book" gets people's attention—they don't even ask what kind of book, or if it is any good. So, I redirected my feeling of doom and gloom to an obsession of writing a "book" during the holiday break.

What I did (Create)

- During any moment that was non-work and non-family, I collated all the rambling emails I have sent you. Then I added more commentary—things I didn't have space for in the emails, other experiences, stuff that could get me in trouble, etc.
- The above took me past Christmas. Then I kind of did a light editing step. But reading my own "book" was rather boring. So I sent off the manuscript to my wife, daughter, and father to gauge how much more effort was warranted. My wife and daughter gave it two half thumbs up. My father was flabbergasted. He said something like "*This* is a *book*?"
- Over weekends after the break, I tinkered a bit more. I stopped after the "Samratisms are going emeritus" email. I didn't want my emails to be influenced by worrying about how they would look in a "book" (kind of a separation of Church and State thing).

Where I am (Delegate)

- Undeterred by my father's skepticism, I decided it was worth the effort to upgrade the "book" from its 9th-grade writing quality. I discovered Karin Wiberg, who helps directionless writers convert their raw content into something more digestible and professional.
- Karin has been cranking away on the manuscript for the last 3-4 weeks. Attached is her status report from this morning. Sure puts many of us to shame when it comes to precision and detail orientation.

- When the manuscript is ready, our marketing team (and maybe the legal team) will take a look to ensure that this thing won't get me fired. I have my wife, daughter, and a trusted colleague lined up to provide feedback (I fired my dad).

What will come next (Procrastinate)

- My best guess is that this "book" will lie in electronic state on my computer for the enjoyment of future Shenbagas.
- At most, I was going to self-publish as that's so easy to do. But then my wife said, "Only bad books get self-published." So I might half-heartedly submit the manuscript to the few publishers who accept manuscripts directly (the trouble of finding an agent is too much). The average book sells only 200 copies. At some point I have to cut my losses on this already heavily negative ROI project.
- I do need a name for the "book." I started with *Book of Sam-ratisms*. That felt too pompous. So the placeholder is *The pandemic journey of a pessimist*. Suggestions more than welcome.[1]

This micro-obsession not only got me through the holiday period but also kept me in high spirits. For many of you who have a few tough weeks ahead, I'd suggest finding an obsession. Maybe you always wanted to learn to cook, sketch, paint, watch all Amitabh Bachchan movies in chronological order... Don't let the laptop and news media consume you. Use this time to do something about which you always said "I wish I could, but I don't have the time for it." Stay safe and healthy. And as always, let me know if I can be of any help.

Samrat

---

[1] My publishing team refused to use the word "pessimist" in the title. And somehow they even tricked me into using the word "optimist." Hmmm.

Figure 1. Editing status report

Dear Samrat,

Happy Friday. I am delighted to report that we end the week 84.2% done with the first pass of editing on your manuscript, with 6,384 of 40,372 words remaining to review. Since you are a consultant, I thought you would appreciate some statistics on the volume and types of revisions thus far, which can be seen in the figure below. (Keep in mind you generated a couple of new chapters to add, which are not included in these totals.)

3092 revisions
Insertions: 1531
Deletions: 1232
Moves: 4
Formatting: 83
Comments: 242

Lest you worry, many of the insertions and deletions consist of punctuation and many of the comments consist of "LOL."

Re timeline, I would anticipate the manuscript to be ready for an internal review by the middle to end of May. Whether you want to share it beyond that is up to you. ☺

Samrat, I must say I am enjoying this manuscript. You have a quirky sense of humor and I anticipate only a few editorial knockdown drag-outs to come.

As always, let me know if you have any questions. Take care, stay healthy, and have a good weekend.

Karin

■ ■ ■

THE NUMBER THIRTEEN gets a bad rap. Hotels and office buildings skip from floor twelve to fourteen. Expectant mothers fret about a due date on the thirteenth and are willing to endure an extra day of pregnancy to avoid the calamity. Cults all around the world look to the sky every Friday the thirteenth to catch a glimpse of the killer meteor streaking through the atmosphere.

In reality we, especially Americans, should be worried about numbers that are a combination of one and nine. Historians rate 1919 as the worst year in America. Just past World War I, this year saw the "Red Scare" bombings, severe race riots, huge strikes, and the president suffering a stroke. Fast forward to 1991 when President George H.W. Bush was lauded for Operation Desert Storm. Little did Americans know at the time that their source of pride had initiated a sequence of events that in ten years would culminate in a devastating tragedy with the events of 9/11. The immediate toll on life was unimaginable, and we will never get a full accounting of the human, emotional, and fiscal cost of the following twenty years of ensuing wars. Finally, we must not forget that two years prior, the 1999 Columbine massacre set the template for many future tragedies where disturbed teens would shoot up their schools and other public venues.

Hence, it should be no surprise that the lifetime-defining virus for billions of humans across the globe was named COVID-19. Other viruses have been more potent in the history of humankind, but none has risen to the level of fame as COVID-19. The reason is simple: COVID-19 found the perfect storm of globalization, news media chasing TRPs,[2] social media looking for viral stories, and elections that featured big personalities.

---

[2] TRP = Television Rating Points or Target Rating Points, a measure that media organizations use when setting prices for advertisers.

As we went through the pandemic, I noticed that the second-most-used word after "COVID" was "unprecedented." Every report started with something along the lines of "we are in an unprecedented situation," "today's numbers are unprecedented," "this year's parade comes during an unprecedented time." After a few weeks I started wondering how long something could be unprecedented before it became precedented. Surely shutting down a salon due to the virus for the second time is not unprecedented—it was already shut down once before! The NFL analysts kept saying it was an unprecedented season. But the MLB and NBA had already completed games and suspended their seasons before the football players even took the field. So, hadn't those leagues set the precedent and thus there was nothing unprecedented for the NFL? These types of random thoughts just kept multiplying in my brain—and I didn't even test positive for COVID-19!

In the middle of all the alarm and chaos, my forty-five-year-old self started looking for the positives in the crisis. To be perfectly clear, I am not looking to minimize the terrible impact this virus has had on the world. Hundreds of thousands have lost their lives, millions have been through terrible suffering, even more will mourn for years the loss of someone close to them, and countless people have been financially devastated. The immense impact of this virus will never be fully understood. However, as we worked through the pandemic, I observed a return to basics for many of us, in both our professional and personal lives. We were all forced to stop for a moment and recognize that life is precious, time with family cannot be taken for granted, and our greatest satisfaction comes from the connections we establish with each other as human beings. Watching TV with family, arguing over which show to pick, pushing everyone to be at the dinner table at the same time, and many other "normal things" that we had relegated to nostalgia on *Leave It to Beaver* episodes made a comeback in real life.

The most clichéd phrase used in the workplace is "we are a

family." In normal circumstances, that is a stretch. I like my colleagues, but I would not donate my left kidney to one as readily as I would to my daughter. But COVID-19 forced many in the workplace to be a family. We got a peek into each other's messy living rooms till everyone figured out the virtual background setting. By the tone of the bark, we could name which dog was getting agitated that their work-from-home owner wouldn't come out to throw the Frisbee. We shared our most intimate daily challenges and were relieved to learn that everyone else was in the same boat. What was unprecedented was that by being physically apart we became emotionally closer.

I have been a lifelong management consultant, with an emphasis on pharmaceuticals and biotech. In essence I help companies figure out how to maximize business performance. I will admit that management consultants are hard-nosed and treat their profession as religion. That was definitely true for me for the twenty years that I pursued client delight, business growth, and professional success with single-minded fervor. But then COVID-19 helped me reset. I realized I was in a people-to-people business. And in a crisis, it served me well to become more vulnerable about my own struggles, dilemmas, and fears. What I share here is inspired by the communications I had with my 600-plus-person team during the course of the pandemic. The team spans multiple geographies, generations, and ethnic backgrounds; nearly three-quarters of my team members are located in India. While I started my communications and emails with the goal of helping, supporting, and maybe even inspiring my team, soon they became a release valve for me.

After having lived through a crisis like COVID-19, I have arrived at the conclusion that business leaders often get paralyzed trying to figure out the ideal message and best way to communicate. They consult with multiple advisors, agonize over how words could be misinterpreted, and often end up not communicating at all. My philosophy became that any communication is better than no communication, and if someone doesn't want to read it, then the delete button is a millisecond away. I share chronologically the emails I sent to my team,[3] my thought process behind them, learnings I feel other business leaders can benefit from, and some of the things I wanted to share but did not in order to keep the emails of manageable size. While the pandemic was the catalyst for my chain of communications, business leaders are faced with a variety of other "crises" all the time. Perhaps when members of my team are faced with one of those in the future, my interactions with them can spark an idea or two.

---

[3] Edited only for things like standardizing punctuation and formatting, anonymizing some names, and a few clarifications that Karin insisted on—and that's the whole point of delegation.

THE LETTERS

Friday, March 13, 2020

To: Compellium Team
From: Samrat Shenbaga
Subject: UPDATE AND DIRECTION FOR
ONGOING CORONAVIRUS SITUATION

All:

We've created an email list (globalcompelliumteam@thefirm.com[4]) that includes everyone with modest activity on Compellium[5] over the last 6 months. I have it in bcc to avoid unintended reply-alls. Many of you won't have ongoing or current engagement with Compellium and can feel free to ignore.

There have been multiple communications from the firm, your local offices, and clients regarding the evolving situation. I wanted to provide guidance from a Compellium perspective.

---

[4] Not a real email address!

[5] Not a real client name! (My legal team wants me to assure you that as a matter of policy we do not identify our clients publicly. Compellium is the fake client name we use for software demos.)

Personal choice

- First and foremost your personal safety and comfort takes priority. Each person will have their own take and personal situation. I might say "I have had malaria, measles, and chicken pox—how bad can this be?" But then others have elderly parents/grandparents or infants at home that are at high risk. And then many just feel uncomfortable based on all the conflicting information. So use your own judgment to make decisions for your situation.

- Do not advise or influence others on how to act. As an example, I cancelled all business travel earlier this week. There are many reasons, but primary was that I didn't want anyone on the Compellium team to think "Oh if the CSL[6] is travelling, I think he is strongly hinting to us that we should too." Be aware of how your actions or words are interpreted by others.

- Be explicit with clients on how they want to engage. Compellium has a ban on non-essential business visitors. Now "non-essential" is being defined differently by different clients. Work with your PAMs[7] and clients to get explicit permission if you need to go in. Of course that is overridden by your personal choice if you don't want to.

Pace of business

- My hunch is that Compellium will go to a work-from-home model in the upcoming days. Many of our other clients have

---

[6] CSL = Client Service Lead. The CSL serves as the person accountable for the relationship between the firm and the client. The CSL has various responsibilities: a) scale their CST (Client Service Team), b) bring the firm's best thinking to the client organization, c) build senior client relationships, d) ensure there is strong collaboration across the CST so that we are building the best solutions for the client, e) tackle tricky situations that arise. I am the CSL for Compellium (reminder: not a real client name!). By the way, consultants love acronyms.

[7] PAMs = Principals, Associate Principals, Managers—in essence, the PAM team is the management team. As I said, consultants like acronyms.

already done it, schools are shutting down, even Disney World in my hometown is closed. That will bring an inevitable slowdown in our business development efforts for a short period of time. But clients still need to get stuff done and I expect we will quickly adapt to the new style. And we have lots of work already in the pipeline that needs to be delivered.

- This "lull" would be a good opportunity to get to things that have been put off. Any process improvements, trainings, etc.

Business continuity

- We have a responsibility to ensure reasonable continuity of our services even during uncertain times. But we are living in an unusual and fast-changing situation. We will conduct a stress test early next week of the most extreme situation— what if all staff had to work from home? This way we can proactively identify problem spots. More details to come.
- An obvious reminder is that working from home doesn't equate to a vacation. ☺ But it will require a different way of working to ensure teams are connected; the best possible technology is available.

Hope that is helpful as you make personal decisions and gives you a sense for steps we are taking on the business. Feel free to write to me with suggestions/thoughts. Thanks much.

Samrat

■ ■ ■

THE ENTIRE LOCKDOWN unraveled in a surreal manner. I equate it to the moment on 9/11 when we heard a plane had crashed into the World Trade Center. All of us assumed that it was an inexperienced amateur pilot who must have made a tragic mistake and hit the tower with a small plane. It was only hours later that the magnitude of the event started sinking in. And even then it was unfathomable what would motivate any human to take such horrific actions.

In retrospect, the beginning of the COVID-19 situation was much the same. When I cancelled my flight, I discussed with my assistant what options we should start considering for two to three weeks down the road. I also worried that Americans were becoming wimpy and that perhaps this was a devious scheme by hand sanitizer manufacturers to boost their quarterly sales. From a business standpoint, it felt like a royal short-term headache to deal with. I had to worry that people would start getting distracted, skip a beat on client delivery, and quickly put us in a situation of fighting fires every day. It was of utmost importance to avoid panic on the team—I didn't need them to be assuming that the business was going to tank and worry about losing their jobs. There was also a delicate dance between showing empathy and reminding them they still had a job to do.

Hence my first salvo was to provide reassurance without giving guarantees and at the same time remind my leadership team they had to lead by example. My dominant focus admittedly was on the health of the business and ensuring we did not dig ourselves into a hole due to short-term panic.

Friday, March 20, 2020

To: Compellium Team
From: Samrat Shenbaga
Subject: REFLECTIONS FROM
FIRST WEEK OF WORK FROM HOME

Compellium Team:

Hope you are all doing well and coping with the fast-evolving global situation. I am extremely proud of how the entire team has rallied to support each other, maintain a high degree of professionalism, and continue to drive client success. This event is a new social experiment for all of us, and everyone has done a commendable job of rising to the occasion. A big thank-you as you work through a period of unprecedented uncertainty.

The fluid situation brings its own load of personal and professional stress. I wanted to share some personal adjustments that I have made—not suggesting that you follow them, but they may spur some ideas.

- I have upped my frequency of contact with many team members and some key clients. Many of these are 15-minute chats. But the goal is to stay connected, check how things are going, and resolve any issues quickly.

- On many of my business calls, I am spending more time socializing. Each person is faced with a different level of stress and it's good for us to act a bit more like friends as opposed to just colleagues, consultants, or clients.
- Working from home always sounds nice till one has to do it all the time! After a couple of days, I was feeling a bit despondent. I felt guilty if I stepped away from my laptop for a few minutes. I missed the general banter with clients and team members in the cafeteria. I was checking news feeds every 10 minutes and there was no good news. You get the drift. So I have been trying a few things.
  - ◻ I step away periodically to get a mental break—watch an episode of a TV show, for example.
  - ◻ To the extent possible, I am fitting personal priorities in. Yesterday I went for a run at 4 pm once I was done with all my calls, knowing that I could finish my emails and deck reviews later in the evening and it wouldn't hold anyone else up.
  - ◻ Lastly I am making quick phone calls to family members or friends I haven't spoken to in a while whenever I am tempted to read the news—they are all stuck at home too. Gives me a break during the workday and is a replacement for the conversations I would typically have with clients or co-workers in the cafeteria.
- I have been using the computer camera. Prior to this event I never did as it made me feel awkward. Now it gives me some sense of normalcy that I can see everyone, gauge body language.
- At the same time the PAM team and I continue to work on ways to improve our ongoing business and find ways to help clients in different ways. Fortunately we are in a business where demand for our services still exists and we

can adapt to the changing needs of clients as well as the situation.

Let us all continue to support each other as we have. Wishing you all the best and good health.

Samrat

■ ■ ■

As WE SLIPPED into an odd world, I started polling my deputies on what they were hearing on the ground. The new working model was mildly inconvenient for me with the need to worry about barking dogs in the background, figuring out how to navigate features of Zoom, and starting to realize that none of my chairs at home was designed to be sat on for more than thirty minutes. Those issues paled in comparison to the problems others on my team were running into. In India, you had three to four people sharing a 700-square-foot apartment with no place to do their individual conference calls. Many in the younger generation were lost on how to navigate basic necessities like food. For eighteen years of their lives their moms had fed them; that was followed by college cafeterias and bars; after college, they graduated to office-provided meals, supplemented by restaurant food purchased with their newfound wealth. Now, all of a sudden, they had to fend for themselves at home. Internet recipes laid out ingredients and utensils that they were hard-pressed to find.

And the hardships of life were being compounded by uncertainty of what the expectations at work were. Is it okay to chitchat, or should we cut straight to work? Is it okay to step away from the computer for lunch? Will I be judged on video calls for the décor in my house? Add to that the growing insecurity around one's job status. In the immediate aftermath of the lockdown, I sensed that people were willing to do anything and everything that was asked of them. No one wanted to be perceived as a whiner or a slacker for fear of being the first in line to be chopped if layoffs came.

Senior leaders can often forget what it was like when they were young and starting their career. A seasoned executive does not immediately panic when unexpected events occur. They know they can reduce overhead costs, freeze hiring, and remove low performers before they see any impact on business performance. Leaders can also assume that because they are not too worried, others will not be either. During a crisis, the first thing a leader must do is go back in time and talk to their twenty-two-year-old self. Many leaders will tell you that they just ask their young employees how they are feeling. Shouldn't that suffice? I can tell you that when I was twenty-two, I never told my boss what was actually on my mind—I told them what I believed they wanted to hear. In order to take meaningful action, a leader must rely on their own market research where the avatar of their own younger self is the most important sample of one. They should have a conversation with that avatar and ensure the young them would like, respect, and listen to the old them. Modify the message as needed!

Another issue is that junior folks tend to feel that their leaders must have all the answers. And in return, the leaders feel they must provide the silver bullet. Rather than giving reassurances and platitudes, it is okay for the leader to let their team know that they, too, have insecurities and are navigating uncharted territory. Perhaps a view into the world of an imperfect leader will help teams feel happier about their own less-than-ideal situation. Personally, I wanted to provide my team some comic relief but struggled with what the right timing would be.

Friday, March 27, 2020

To: Compellium Team
From: Samrat Shenbaga
Subject: THE CONTINUED ADAPTATION TO
CHANGES IN LIFE DUE TO CORONAVIRUS

Compellium Team:

 We are at the end of another week the likes of which few have experienced before. I am running out of "un" words to describe it—unusual, unprecedented, unsettling, unbelievable... But as we settle into this new reality I am also experiencing some "ful" feelings. This week it is "thankful." So why thankful?

- I am thankful that, to the best of my knowledge, the Compellium team, their loved ones, our firm's employees, and their families (including mine) are all safe and healthy.
- I am thankful that I am part of a team that deeply cares for one another. We are finding ways to support each other in keeping spirits up. I hear of stories of virtual happy hours, funny videos being circulated, and unrelated team members helping others with very basic things. The PAMs always

discuss the health of the team with me first, and then the business at hand.

- I am thankful that we are finding ways to help Compellium support patients[8] through these difficult times. Projects are being launched on determining how to ensure continued care of cancer patients, how to still launch new products which are critical for patient care.

- I am thankful (oddly) that my biggest personal problem is the inability to get a haircut as all the hair salons are closed. If the salon closures last another 3 weeks, alas I will rival Boris Johnson for messiest hair 😞 (fresh on my mind as I watched his video this morning about a positive test).

At the same time, I recognize this is a time of high stress for many of us. This is the first week of a national lockdown for a majority of the team, in India. Having grown up in New Delhi, I was at the epicenter of the 1984 riots,[9] the Mandal Commission unrest,[10] and the Babri Masjid carnage[11] (for which unfortunately I was traveling in a near-empty train from Kharagpur to Delhi right as the riots broke out—some of my college friends actually felt it was a good idea to raise the train shutters to see what was going on in UP[12] 😊). But those were localized to certain geographies and during the days when viral, alarmist news did not travel through WhatsApp. So I can only imagine the amplified stress many of you feel as you are disconnected from family and friends with so much uncertainty around you. With that, I have a few **requests** of you:

---

[8] Recall we work in the pharmaceutical space.

[9] After the assassination of Indian Prime Minister Indira Gandhi.

[10] A commission set up in India in 1979 to redress caste discrimination; its attempt to implement recommendations in 1990 led to protests.

[11] Babri Masjid was a mosque built in 1528–29 and demolished by Hindu nationalists in 1992, an incident that led to violence across the Indian subcontinent.

[12] UP = Uttar Pradesh, the state where Babri Masjid was located; the state has since been split in two.

- Take the mental breaks you need.
- Reach out to fellow team members and PAMs for support on anything. Don't place all the pressure on yourself. For example, your internet connection might go down. Rather than stress about not being able to get a file out, call your project manager to discuss a solution. There are more options that you will each individually be aware of.
- But the above does not have to be restricted just to work matters. If you are feeling a heightened sense of anxiety, utilize team members and the firm's help line as part of your support network.

Remember we are all in this together and will come out stronger. Wishing you all good health. As always, do not hesitate to reach out to me with anything on your mind.

Samrat

■ ■ ■

THE REALIZATION SLOWLY started dawning on many business leaders that the new work situation could be a protracted phenomenon. WFH (work from home) popped up in every other communication (I found it amusing that during a quick scan of emails, WFH could easily be misread as WTF). At that point, "protracted" was defined as four to six weeks—maybe a couple months—but no more. The din of the news media was reaching a feverish pitch and all of us found ourselves tracking every "breaking news" item—and worse still, kept forwarding them along to anyone and everyone in our contact list. Young people who spent much of their life on smartphones were suddenly inundated with more alarming information than they could possibly handle. Personally, I stuck to my usual pattern of news gathering—watch CNN for five minutes and be told the apocalypse was upon us, then switch over to Fox News for another five minutes to be told that the whole virus was a mainstream media conspiracy, and then move to Google and type "what the hell is actually going on?" Over the years, journalists have become entertainers in desperate search of clicks and exposure. With their massive psychographic research capabilities, I am convinced that all media organizations have come to the conclusion that "fear and gloom" sells. The goal of every so-called news program seems to be to take the most egregious outlier and paint it as the overwhelming reality.

The need to lend a hopeful voice in the midst of all this doom and gloom felt like a grand necessity. While I had analytically surveyed the news stations to conclude that each one was exaggerating a different version of the truth, I suspected not everyone on my team followed my analytical rigor. Maybe it would help to steer everyone towards the middle. The reality of the situation was not pretty—but it was not as if we had a life-ending meteor hurtling towards us.

Around this time, I began to recognize that frequency of communication might not be enough. Content was becoming more important as well. Given that I was the leader of the team, I had to be the "adult" in the (virtual) room. In these situations, it is important for the team leader to portray calm and balance. At the same time, one cannot be seen as distant and aloof. Just prior to the lockdown, I had participated in a leadership development exercise. While I fared well on many dimensions, my biggest challenge was "intimacy" with the team—many people found my seniority to be intimidating. I will admit that being intimate does not come naturally in my family. My daughter is mortified if I try to hug her, hence we just bump fists. Strangely, the virtual world gave me more courage to throw out what was on my mind.

In order to climb the virtual emotion wall, I decided to venture boldly into the world of . . . emojis. I always considered emojis as unprofessional in a business setting and if used, then more than one in an email seemed like an admission of complacency. After all, if one's writing was truly funny, what need is there to insert a smiley emoji? However, I knew most on my team were in their mid-twenties and things that might strike me as funny could be wildly disturbing to them. Sensitivity has risen to what seems to me almost ludicrous levels at times; it seems one is bound to offend at least 5 percent of readers no matter what, and that possibility did give me pause. The last thing I wanted was to be called on the carpet by the chief HR officer because some twenty-two-year-old felt I was making light of riots in India that occurred twenty-five years ago. But when I sanitized my emails, even *I* was bored reading them. So, I made the decision to read twice, and if the content didn't seem likely to end up as incriminating evidence in a newspaper exposé, then I hit send. I broke my emoji business rule to help the reader differentiate where I was being serious and where I was just riffing. And I steeled myself with resolve that I wouldn't stop communicating to the 95 percent who would appreciate a gesture simply for fear of the 5 percent.

An immediate goal for me was to reduce the stress of the pressure cooker environment many team members were creating for themselves. The situation we were in was not created by us or being experienced only by us. A global problem often commands universal compassion, but individuals still worry about being seen as weak if they can't battle through the adversity. I wanted my team to know that they were not alone and that they should not feel they had to make all the hard decisions themselves. Everyone was in the same boat they were, and together we could get through these tricky waters.

Friday, April 3, 2020

To: Compellium Team
From: Samrat Shenbaga
Subject: AN ATTEMPT TO MAINTAIN NORMALCY

Compellium Team:

We are at the close of another week. I am getting tired of many things but will never get tired of repeating that I am proud of how you continue to support each other and clients. It is a real testament to your personal value system. Each week comes with some new learnings. This week I decided that I should try to maintain some normal routines—I've found it to be quite refreshing. Thought I'd share a few ways I am doing this (and adapt to your own situation if you like):

- I wear a tie and dress shirt as I always do during business hours. It is helping me separate my work life from my home life.
- I have had a long-standing ritual with my 8th-grade daughter. When I am traveling, I send her a text in the morning wishing her the best with the day in school and at the end

of the day I check on how things went. Now she is also "working from home." But we still exchange the daily texts even though we are under the same roof. Gives us a bit of levity.

- Biggest thing of all, I took a vacation day today. ☺ I realized that I had skipped the 2-3 days that were planned in March and typically I wouldn't have gone almost 2 months without a small break. Luckily for me the golf course is open but one has to walk it. While I am sore from 7 miles of walking and my golf score has gotten worse, I feel great. So take a day off just as you always would and recharge the batteries (my only request is that not all of you take off on the same day ☺).

On a more serious note, many on the team have also raised the important question of "When the world is facing an existential crisis, should we really be practicing commerce/doing BD[13]/doing market research, etc., etc.?" Very good question and I do not have a great answer. But the way I think of it (and I expect each of us has our own lens):

- Much as I would like to go out and physically help, that would only make the situation worse. So I help in smaller ways (primarily through charitable contributions).
- It is important to keep the economic engine running. As Compellium CSL, my biggest responsibility is to keep 300+ firm employees gainfully employed. They in turn support the livelihood of at least 10x the number of people and so on...
- While sometimes it can sound like a stretch, our work does have an impact on patient health. Right now we are helping Compellium understand how they continue to get critical

---

[13] BD = Business Development, a.k.a. sales.

medication to patients. We are an important engine to enable Compellium to make life-saving decisions during a turbulent time.

■ And lastly, if I didn't work then I would just go nuts listening to the news.

With that, I wish you all good health and hope you relax the mind and body over the weekend. As always, feel free to reach out to me with anything. Take care.

Samrat

■ ■ ■

I WAS ONE OF THE YOUNGEST ever to be elected to partner at my firm (at the age of thirty-two). A large driver of the rapid progression was that I managed to skip a couple of levels within the promotion ladder. Each of these rungs was introduced just after I had leapt over them. If they had been in place, then it would have easily added at least four more years to my climb. Everyone strives for quick progression. Unfortunately, when you achieve it, you are out of place very quickly. I was the kid in a group of much more seasoned partners. Clients found it hard to take advice seriously from someone who was two decades younger than they were. I could sense them thinking, "How much experience could this guy possibly have?"

In order to be taken seriously, I decided to age myself. Men in my family gray young. Rather than color my hair, I let it gray out. That helped but still left me looking like an old young man. Hence, the next step was to look stodgy and old-fashioned. Till the age of thirty-five, I had worn a tie once a year to the holiday party. My wife had tied the knot many years prior, and I carefully moved it up and down as an annual ritual. Perhaps a move to daily tie-wearing would make me look like a Serious Executive. As I delved into the market for ties, I was amazed to see the various patterns, design styles, and textures. The act of wearing a tie definitely increased my street cred. But it also became an obsession as I looked for the best colors to match my shirts and patterns to suit different occasions (such as the bald eagle tie for patriotic days, the dog with newspaper in mouth for times I thought of my dogs, the orange bat tie for Halloween, and so on). Before I knew it, and aided by ties becoming the gift of choice I received for every occasion, I had over two dozen ties.[14] So now the tie has become a standard part of my attire and brings a certain degree of normalcy, like putting on my school uniform when I was a kid.

During uncertain times, teams pay attention to every small move their leader makes. I figured that by wearing a tie, in addition to maintaining a sense of normalcy for myself, I could project the same for everyone on my team. If I had moved down to T-shirts and sweats, I worried the team would take that as a sign of the world coming apart.

A month into lockdown, ethical dilemmas began to emerge for the younger generation. Young management consultants on my team started soul-searching about whether they were really living up to their social responsibility in this crisis. The emotional reaction was "should we be making all this money while the world is going through such suffering?" I had a decision to make. Either I could tell them to shut up and get back to work. Or I could be gently honest that there were no good answers and the best way to get through this period was to keep their focus on what was in front of them. Otherwise they risked driving themselves and everyone around them crazy.

---

[14] One of my team members recently asked what the latest tie count was—it stands at fifty-three.

I also didn't want to pander. Consultants are notorious for over-stating the impact of their work. It is true that we make a posi-tive change to businesses and the customers they serve. But you'll find consultants indiscriminately describe their work using terms like "transform," "revolutionize," or "leapfrog." When a consultant says that to a clueless family member, it sounds cool. If a consultant says it to another consultant, then the BS meter hits all-time highs. In order to be credible with my team, I decided to stretch a little but not too much.

Friday, April 10, 2020

To: Compellium Team
From: Samrat Shenbaga
Subject: APPLYING AN OPTIMISTIC LENS

Compellium Team:

We have another week under our belt. I repeat how proud I am of all of you. The incredible job you continue to do in support of each other and clients never ceases to amaze. As this week went by, I was reminded of a book my father (copied above) asked me to read when I was a teenager. It was titled *The Power of Positive Thinking.* My memory is fuzzy, but I recall my father calling me an "eternal pessimist." I never saw the glass as being half empty but rather it was always totally shattered! Many years later I described the story to a fellow principal. He remarked, "You are not a pessimist; you are just a realist!" I suppose one can look at the same situation/facts and interpret based on one's perspective.

With that in mind, I adopted a positive lens to things I experienced this week:

- I visit a website called Worldometer (worldometers.info) to track the stats on the virus. The site collects data from public sources across the globe. There is no commentary, and one can derive their own conclusions. They even have log and linear curves. My personal take is there would appear to be **some glimmer of hope for flattening the curve in many places**. The data scientists in the group are welcome to go crazy with the data over the weekend.

- Earlier this week about 10 of my cousins who I have not met in years (~15) decided to do a Zoom call. A customary Indian tradition is that when you see someone after many years, you say, "Wow, you have not changed. You look the same as ever." When confronted with the comment during the Zoom call, my natural instinct was to think, "Wow, I must have looked really old 15 years ago." But I shifted my lens and convinced myself that **I have discovered the fountain of youth.**

- My wife found paper towels on Amazon. Enough said.

- My comrade in hair, Boris, ended up in the ICU. But it is terrific that he is making a steady recovery. Boris will now become the first country leader to be immune to the virus even though he did it the hard way!

- I went into a bit of a sneezing spell on Wednesday. Never was I so happy to be sneezing, because it is not a symptom of the virus (at least that's what Google says). **Thank you, allergies.**

- Last but not least, the Compellium account had its best ever financial month in March. I can't share numbers here as my dad is not covered by a CDA.[15] 😶 We still have to keep working at it, but **all your hard work is driving great impact.**

---

[15] Confidential Disclosure Agreement, sometimes known as Nondisclosure Agreement (NDA).

At a time when there is a lot of bad news around us, let's look for some positives. As the pandemic continues, all of us are becoming aware of people directly or indirectly affected. Let's continue to do what we can to support each other and others around us.

If you are bored, feel free to write to my dad (his email address is on the cc line). From the number and length of his recent WhatsApp messages, I can assure you he has a lot of time on his hands to respond. ☺ Take care and stay healthy. As always let me know of questions/comments/suggestions.

Samrat

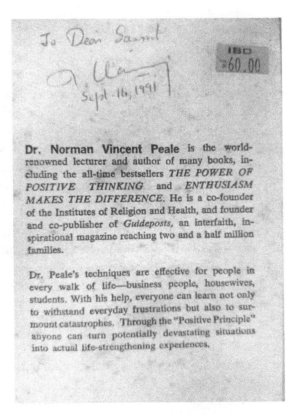

Figure 2. The copy of *The Power of Positive Thinking* given to me by my father

■ ■ ■

THE JOB DONE by governments to communicate the objective of the lockdowns can at best be rated a C+. Most of us believed (and were told) that the lockdowns would make the virus disappear, when in fact the goal was to give health systems a fighting chance to catch up. Also, given that no one had experienced an event such as this in their lifetime, calibrating it to anything else proved to be tough. I was of the mindset that a month was already much longer than anything I had imagined in my wildest mental models and surely we were approaching the end quickly. With that in mind, I began looking for any glimmers of hope. Worldometer was an addictive drug to an analytically oriented person. It constantly updated virus counts and death counts by state and country. Not only that, but it also normalized the statistics by population. I would check it every fifteen minutes to gauge how that day's numbers were going to end up. I started recognizing cyclical patterns based on reporting within the week and realized that one can't get too excited by Monday's numbers as hospitals don't report on Sundays. I ignored all news coverage and Fauci updates and made Worldometer my bible.

I know I am not an optimist. But I am not sure if I am a pessimist either. And even if I am a pessimist, I don't understand why it is qualified as a negative trait. It is the equivalent of implying that being short is a bad thing. Show me one tall jockey.

For me, being a pessimist is a positive. It shows that I don't take success for granted, am always going to be looking for the next idea to compensate for the supposed failure of my previous one, and will be constantly worried that everything I have worked for could go away overnight. Some pessimists curl up in a ball and give up; others paddle frantically all the time because they are afraid of drowning. If I were to believe that everything would go swimmingly well, then there is a high probability I would quit trying. In golf, I started with the objective of getting the ball off the ground consistently. That took me two months. But did I stop there? No. I moved to hitting the ball consistently forward. Once I was able to do that (three months later), I shifted to aiming to keep the ball in the same hole I was playing. And then to staying on the fairway, to making the green in under ten shots, to breaking 120 under my own rules, and so on. If I were an optimist, I would still be on the driving range waiting to get to the perfect swing.

But I do recognize that it takes my conscious effort to see the positives in a forest of negatives. So, I work to find the positives and enjoy them for a short minute. During COVID-19, finding positives became difficult even with a lot of effort. But I didn't want my team to give up. If I could do it, then surely they could.

Good leaders have to live with a sense of healthy paranoia. Running any business is an uphill climb. The positive is that when one reaches the summit, the view is beautiful. But the problem is that the view also reveals taller mountains ahead, and if one takes just one step backwards, then they can go tumbling down the slope they just finished climbing. Injecting that paranoia into team members is important, but if done in too large a dose, it can lead to mass panic, and then the team falls apart. Perhaps the easiest thing to do is to be transparent and honest—everyone knows life is not always a bed of roses.

Friday, April 17, 2020

To: Compellium Team
From: Samrat Shenbaga
Subject: LEARNING BUSINESS LESSONS
WHILE WORKING FROM HOME

Compellium Team:

Another week is nearly behind us and now (at least for me) the new work style is beginning to feel more like the norm. As always, I am extremely proud of your dedication, focus, and empathy for others. This week I realized that learnings in my personal life can be directly applied to how I manage clients and the business (or serve as helpful reminders).

As background, I had planned on a half-day vacation on Thursday so that I could hit the golf course. As luck would have it, storms rolled in overnight and lingered all day long. Noticing that I had some time on my hands, my wife asked that I vacuum parts of the house. Like many others, we have temporarily suspended housekeeping services to enable effective social distancing. While my expertise in vacuuming is limited, I figured it couldn't be that hard. In the following 60 minutes I learned a few lessons.

- **_Determining scope upfront is important..._** As I looked around the house, it did not seem like a big job. I figured at most it would be a 20-minute exercise. But I failed to account for the stairs, curves, changes involved in different flooring materials, the fact that the vacuum cleaner cord doesn't go too far, etc., etc. Hence, my 20-minute estimate was off by a factor of at least 2x.

- **_...but clients love scope creep._** When the project was proposed to me, my wife only included a couple of the more heavily traveled areas in the specifications. But as I got started the narrative changed to "Now that you are at it anyway, why not just knock off a few other things?" Closets started opening up, dining chairs were moved so that I could get into crevices under the table, bathrooms got added to the list. I discovered at least one closet that I never knew existed.

- **_Some people want the credit but not the responsibility._** The one room that was (surprisingly) in good shape was my daughter's bedroom. The floor showed no sign of dust. As I pondered various hypotheses, I realized that while my daughter proudly claims both of our Labrador retrievers to be "her pets," she never lets them into her room. And they are responsible for 95% of the dirt in the house that comes in every time they return from the backyard. Now that I think of it, she may not even know the dogs' names. 😟

- **_Always ask for help when you don't know what you are doing._** As I moved to a room that was carpeted, I found that the vacuum was sucking at it hard. I could almost feel the carpet rising off the subfloor. I tried many adjustments to the speed and intensity of the machine and shoved it harder but to no avail. Finally, I texted my wife asking how to resolve the issue. She pointed me to another closet which had a special attachment for carpets—problem solved. Who

knew vacuum cleaners have as many attachments as there
are irons in my golf bag?

As you can see, home life and work life are really blending together now. I wrote about optimism last week. Last night my optimism increased as reports of Gilead's great remdesivir clinical trial data emerged. Hopefully we will have an intermediate solution while scientists work on the vaccine. But an even bigger victory for me—I got a confirmation email just now that *a pair of hair clippers has actually shipped.* ☺ I need to take a day off next week to diligently study the operating manual, watch YouTube instruction videos, and perhaps experiment on my dogs—else I risk repeating vacuuming-type mistakes that will be far more visible.

Wishing you a good weekend and good health. Take care.

Samrat

■ ■ ■

IN SOME WAYS, a pandemic is a great equalizer (and in other ways just the opposite). By mid-April we had entered the zone where the most basic tasks that we had put off could no longer be ignored, and people who had previously outsourced tasks to others were now forced to figure them out for themselves.

Vacuuming definitely brought its challenges. It is remarkable how inversely correlated the aesthetic look of furniture is with the ability to clean it. There is an incredibly unnecessary number of bends and corners that just collect dust. And the more you look, the more you find. I couldn't believe the dust accumulation under the bed or the numerous spots where popcorn could roll. My immediate conclusion was that I needed to use "minimal applicable standards." If it looked good on the surface, it was good enough—the professionals would do a deep clean eventually.

And my hair was a source of constant stress. For weeks I had held out hope that salons would reopen and I would be able to get a professional haircut. Once it was clear that any possibility of entering a salon was at least weeks away, it was time to spring into action. As I began taking on the tasks of vacuuming and hair styling, the role of expertise in any profession became abundantly clear. I must have spent at least six hours researching different hair trimmers and an equal amount of time viewing YouTube videos on how to use them. The combination of different clipper sizes, the exact height to go to, and how to smooth out edges all felt quite complicated. The saving grace was that a computer camera only catches a few angles of one's face. Given that there was very limited human-to-human interaction, there was little need to worry if a chunk of hair got chopped off on the back of my head. Once I got past the clippers, the next concern was hair dye. The product website had a dazzling array of colors. I am lucky to have black hair[16] (or I should say I "need" black hair). So, I just went with the darkest variation with the assumption that any discrepancies would be mitigated by Zoom.

During this time, I felt it was important to convey to my team that all our lives looked quite similar now. On paper it might appear that I had access to more resources than most of them did, but that didn't mean I could outsource my problems. On the contrary, my financial resources had led to an accumulation of stuff that now needed care I was not qualified to provide. A part of me worried that complaining about vacuuming or asking advice from my wife on the topic would be seen as sexist. But I stuck with my "what the heck" attitude. From the few notes I would get in response to my emails, people seemed to find comfort in the communications. And I figured it was easy enough to hit the delete button if someone found them annoying.

---

[16] Now that I am on the wrong side of forty, I no longer have to strive to not look like the kid in the group, but rather the opposite.

Friday, April 24, 2020

To: Compellium Team
From: Samrat Shenbaga
Subject: SOME THINGS THAT
STICK WITH YOU FOREVER

Compellium Team:

Another solid week in the books. You continue to fill me with pride and joy by being great colleagues, great business consultants, and most importantly good, decent human beings. My waist size luckily has held steady in the last couple of months despite incessant snacking, but my chest size keeps going up as it fills up further every week with the thrill of being part of this team.

You might recall I copied my dad a couple of weeks ago. As with everything else in life, he sent me a lot of feedback with the key point being "don't you think these young folks find you being preachy?" My response was "I don't care. They have no other choice. No one listens to me at home anyway—so let me try here." This week I found myself going back to some of my "comfort spots." Some things, for whatever reason, just stick with you and influence how you manage professional and personal dilemmas.

■ **Old is not bad.** I watch a lot of movies. My philosophy is: Why read a book when it is summarized in a 2-hour movie? With the recent situation, I caught up on the newer movies (especially in Hindi and Tamil). Within one week I had exhausted all the 5-star-rated movies, and by week 4 I was down to the 2.5-stars. Right now I am trying to get through *Samrat & Co.* in 15-minute chunks—great title, terrible movie. As I got tired of the new stuff, I went back to two movies that I have likely watched at least 15 times in the last couple of years.

□ *The Hunt for Red October:* My favorite Hollywood movie of all time. Any submarine movie made since then takes inspiration from this one. Sean Connery is just amazing in it. The movie always strengthens my belief that ***anything said in a British/Scottish accent just sounds brilliant***. So if you have it, then maximize its potential! More importantly, substance is king—and as long as we continue delivering impeccable outputs to our clients they will keep coming back.

□ *Jaane Bhi Do Yaaro:* This is a Hindi movie from the early 1980s. The budget was one million rupees, or probably $30k then. Think of the talent pool in this movie as Indian equivalents of Gary Oldman, Ed Norton, Jeff Bridges, and Helena Bonham Carter— but before anyone knew of them. It features hard satire on the blatant corruption in India at the time. One scene that I watch repeatedly is when a corrupt contractor complains about his competitor. He says, "Hum cement mein reth milate hain, woh tho reth mein cement milata hai." Translation: "All I do is mix sand into the cement to adulterate it; that guy mixes cement into sand." The irony is never lost on me. I often think of it when I just want to smile at the irony playing out in front of me. Recently I heard a complaint about the firm wanting a rate adjustment and I thought to myself, "Prices go up on everything every year; why wouldn't our prices go up too?" Sometimes it is good to recognize that **there are contradictions all around us, and not all are worth arguing over.** You will find them all around you now. Be cognizant of which ones you really want to delve into. If you let each one trouble you, then it is easy to lose your mind.

- **Don't blame the listener; evaluate what you are saying.** Some of you may know of Paul (copied above); he was RMP[17] for Europe and CSL for one of our biggest clients. One time Paul was on stage at a company-wide summit. He said in his opening, "I am not going to ask you guys to turn off your phones and close your laptops. If I am an interesting presenter and have anything useful to say, then you will automatically do that. But if I am no good, then it is fair game for you to use your time the way you see fit." Paul said that in less than 30 seconds, but it has stuck with me forever. So in today's crazy world, don't feel compelled to attend every meeting you are invited to (including those I schedule)—it is the responsibility of the person proposing the meeting to make it worth your time.

- **Simplicity is often the most satisfying.** After a few weeks of fancy cooking experiments being tried in my house, I returned to a simple childhood staple of mine—yogurt rice and plantain chips. To every Westerner (like my wife), that might sound "disgusting" as my daughter describes it. My North Indian friends always called it a "wimpy meal." But for

---

[17] RMP = Region Managing Principal. RMPs have geographic management responsibility (Europe, Asia, and so on) and ensure that things are in place so the consultants can do their jobs.

a Tamilan it is pure bliss. There are lots of things coming at us fast and furious right now—task forces, reviews, meetings, annoying CSL emails. But the best thing we can do is stay laser-focused on the task at hand. *So if anyone is pulling you into things that cause unwanted distraction, let me know and I will help you get out of it.*
Got a bit long here. Stay healthy and safe.
Samrat

■ ■ ■

CLIENTS HIRE MANAGEMENT consultants for their expertise in solving many types of problems, operational efficiency being one of the top issues. Consultants are effective at dissecting the areas of potential "fat" within the client organization, providing clear recommendations, and helping clients deal with the ensuing disruption. However, within their own organizations consultants can fall victim to the same issues they fix for their clients. They tell clients that their processes are too heavy; meanwhile, they add new committees without assessing which existing ones should be consolidated or eliminated. They express dismay about how clients take four months to decide their budgets for the coming year, and then they kick off their own annual planning exercise in July. For an impatient person like me, I start wondering why we can't apply a dose of our medicine to ourselves. After all, practicing on ourselves what we preach to others would be the best way to learn.

As a team leader, it is important to recognize these contradictions but also to be judicious in calling them out. If I were to go after every one of them, I'd be an outcast in no time. Sometimes "chuckle and ignore" is a good strategy. But at the expense of being a killjoy, I have found it important to raise my observation of "consultant hypocrisy" with my peers and team members. After all, a successful consultant can quickly become an arrogant consultant, who can even more quickly become an out-of-demand consultant.

When I sent this email out, I debated including a small story that demonstrated why consultants needed to be humble, but the note was already getting too long so I skipped it. However, to illustrate the point: A good friend of mine is a litigation attorney. After winning a big case, he bought a flashy new Porsche 911. While admiring the car, I asked whether he would drive this car to his clients' offices, or if he would stick with his old Lexus. He said to me, "If I pull up to a client with the 911, they know how good I am. On the other hand, if *you* show up at your client with this car, they will immediately wonder how much you are overcharging them!" That is the life of a consultant in a nutshell.

One note on the email: Somehow I landed on the phrase "pride and joy" in the first couple of sentences and it became a staple of all subsequent communications. I suspect there was some amount of laziness involved, where I got tired of saying thank-you in different ways or pointing out successes the team had had. When we were all dealing with computer-screen fatigue, I didn't want to make emails any longer than they needed to be. But the phrase was truly reflective of how I felt, and at the same time it allowed me to quickly pivot to the main points I wanted to make. In my mind "pride" related to business outcomes and impact the team was driving. And "joy" was an all-encompassing feeling; it sounded a little more substantial than "happy," which might be seen as insensitive during a pandemic. Perhaps it was a little sappy, but it did the trick.

Friday, May 1, 2020

To: Compellium Team
From: Samrat Shenbaga
Subject: OKAY, THESE THINGS ARE
REALLY BEGINNING TO BUG ME

Compellium Team:

That's a full month in the history books. As always, you fill me with more pride and joy than you could ever imagine. But that is the last positive thing I am going to say. I've been trying to maintain a positive tone every week—after all that's what the cover page of every leadership book says is expected of a "Leader." But come on, some things are just getting out of control. And next time you experience any of the below craziness, feel free to say *"Samrat says enough is enough."*

I have had it up to here with Zoom shaming.

When this whole thing started ~6 weeks ago, it was quite nice to reconnect with everyone on camera, take a peek at what their houses and apartments looked like, comment on how cute it was that their baby was bawling in the background or that their dog was barking away, and just in general be glad that they looked alive and healthy. But some people have taken it way too far.

- **The Zoom camera-shaming people need to knock it off.** Lately I notice that all the cameras are off at the beginning of a call. Then inexplicably one person decides to turn theirs on. What does that imply? It says "What's wrong with all you other people? I turned mine on, and now you are just being poor sports." One by one everyone else slowly turns on. There is always the smart one who is like "I don't know what's going on with my camera settings. It just won't come on. Let me call tech support after this." Hey look, I get invited to a lot of meetings. And by the powerful law of the normal distribution, half of them are just plain boring (said law does not apply to calls I organize). In the pre-virus days, I would just get on the phone, put it on mute, keep the camera off, eat my hot dog, check my texts, catch up on TMZ, unmute every 7 minutes and say something like "I agree" or "That's a good idea." ***Please, please, let us go back to the old Zoom days.*** I propose a rule that everyone has to agree to turn on their cameras.

- **No one really believes you are sitting on a beach in Hawaii.** What's up with all these virtual backgrounds? Let's think about who sees the background—not the person who puts them up, given that it is supposedly behind them, but poor me for whom the image is projected all over my laptop. And do I really need to get aggravated looking at a beach in Hawaii when I know that the only way to get there right now is on a canoe like the Polynesians did 1,500 years ago???? And how come these virtual backgrounds have no people in them—were they created after a lockdown went into effect? ***Unfreakingbelievable.***

- **And stop giving people heart attacks by putting up an office background.** I almost fell over when someone appeared to be sitting in an empty Pune office. I wondered what type of crazy dedication spurs one to risk their life to come into the office in the middle of a global pandemic. Luckily it was just another wild background idea where apparently all other office workers had left except for the one I was speaking with.

Just because I am home doesn't mean I don't have a life.

On Wednesday I was sitting on my couch at 8 pm, doing absolutely nothing. My wife came around and said, "Why don't you just put up those paintings that have been sitting in boxes for the last two years. All you are doing is sitting at home. I've been asking you to do it for the last 18 months." *Wait a minute.* If there were no darn virus, I would be sitting at a hotel bar, eating a turkey BLT with waffle fries, washing them down with a couple of Old Fashioneds, while watching a meaningless early season MLB game and unsuccessfully explaining to some random person what I do for a living. So me being home doesn't change a thing. I am not getting off that couch.

Maybe it has happened to you, but once in a while I hear from another staffer something like "You are home, so maybe you can take this call at 7 am or 9 pm." *I don't think so.* I didn't do that before the virus and I am not doing it now. This type of request is the equivalent of asking the Pune employees to give up their precious 15 minutes in the morning they use to clean up their text messages while waiting for the elevator. And for those who haven't figured it out yet: you first have to take the elevator down to the garage, ride it back up, and enjoy the disappointed looks of all the people patiently waiting on the ground floor when the door opens and they realize there is no room.

Good talk. Stay safe and healthy, and do your time entry. And don't post mean things about me on Blowfish.[18]

Samrat

---

[18] This is humorous if you know what Fishbowl is. If you don't, read the next footnote.

■ ■ ■

ONCE THE SHOCK of the pandemic and lockdowns started to wear
off, the flood of "best practices" advice came at us from all direc-
tions. Companies were facing a kind of uncertainty they had never
experienced before, which appeared to trigger an overreaction in
many quarters. Administrators frantically tried to gauge the need for
contingency plans. Broadcast calls were hosted on the importance of
giving employees breaks and reducing their stress levels, and insisting
that work not be taken on if it would lead to slightly longer hours.
You couldn't log on to LinkedIn without someone opining on the
best way to reduce mental fatigue, increase productivity, and motivate employees. Everyone became an expert on human behavior
and interactions. The mere job of reducing stress for everyone was
sending the stress levels of management teams into the stratosphere.

The majority of the noise was well intended—just frustratingly
uncoordinated within many companies. In organizations, HQ has
to establish some common norms or else there's chaos. However,
local situations are different, and uniform application of the same
rules and mechanisms can prove to be counterproductive. Organizations can take a page from the structure of the government:
the federal government provides essential services like defense and
infrastructure, and then state governments make choices about how
to shape various initiatives based on local cultures and needs. HQ
can offer "federal" guidelines, but individual business leaders must
then act as "governors" to make the right decisions for the situation
on the ground in their local team, office, or region. The frustration
was building at all levels. And it was making people snappy.

Someone on my leadership team mentioned that I was trend-
ing on a professional network called "Fishbowl"[19] as a result of my

_____

[19] The cool kids already know what Fishbowl is, but my editor did not. It is a social
media site for workplace conversations and advice.

emails. On hearing the news, I had a near nervous breakdown as I did not want the HR team all over me, asking to review and approve my communications. The managers on my team told me that the commentary was incredibly positive compared to most other posts on the site.

Out of curiosity I downloaded the app. It didn't take me long to determine that I was a dinosaur when it came to navigating modern-day social media apps. From what I could decipher, most of the mentions about me were in jest (whew, relief), but people also appeared to look forward to my Friday emails, as though they couldn't believe a senior partner would go out on a limb and be less businesslike (copying my dad on an email was a big hit).

What was disturbing was the incredible number of posts about the anger people felt with the cacophony of incoherent messages coming at them—and this was true of every "bowl" regardless of which company or professional group it was for. I couldn't fault them—it was an understandable reaction—and I had a choice to make. The textbook management tactic would be to provide solace to the team and explain to them why the party line was the best one and how we all had to hold hands and get along. Then on a whim I thought, "To heck with it—I am just going to mirror their negative sentiment. Maybe a negative multiplied by a negative will lead to a positive." But as a leader in the firm, I couldn't just go "full Monty." Inserting a degree of humor while still recognizing the problem was the key.

There was a noticeable change within my team after this email. First, I got many replies thanking me profusely. People were relieved that they were not breaking a sacred rule by not turning on the camera. Not needing to worry about how they looked or what people might think of their decorating taste reduced stress immensely. The virtual backgrounds did stay but got more professional (or boring). And most importantly, I noticed that many team members got comfortable marking some slots on their calendar as "not available." I may have started that trend when I blocked my calendar till 8:30 a.m. It was a genuine need, as my dogs require a lot of management in the morning. When I travel, I don't have to deal with the problem, but when home, everything from dogs to trash to picking up the mail becomes a responsibility I can't just reject.

The greater lesson was that when leaders portray constant positivity, there is a point after which they lose credibility. No one believes that anyone can be that chirpy and optimistic all the time. A good dose of negativity does the heart some good. It also creates an intangible bond across the team as everyone realizes that problems are omnipresent.

Leaders should rely on their firm to provide them with guidance but should not accept it as the law of the land. As Captain Barbossa famously says in one of the *Pirates of the Caribbean* movies, "The [pirate's] code is more what you would call 'guidelines' than actual rules." Each team leader must review their company-provided "code," decide what parts must be strictly followed, throw out sections that don't apply, and modify others as needed.

Friday, May 8, 2020

To: Compellium Team
From: Samrat Shenbaga
Subject: GUIDELINES I FIND HELPFUL IN LIFE &
WORK—USE WITH EXTREME CAUTION

Compellium Team:

We have wrapped up another good week. I experience the feeling of pride and joy each and every day by being part of your team. Last week a response to my email prompted me to finish out *Samrat & Co.* on my 5th attempt. In the movie, the main character uses "Samratisms" to express his philosophies in life. I have many of my own "Samratisms," and for your consideration I share the top two that have influenced choices in my personal and professional life.

- **Aim low and you will never disappoint yourself.** As evidence I attach results of a survey I conducted with my wife (copied above) and daughter to rate their experience with the cleaning services I have been providing during COVID-19. Market researchers will argue that the sample size is too low, but they need to realize that the results represent 100%

of the population. When I issued the survey, I expected extremely negative feedback. But you will see there is a lot of green[20] in it, especially when it comes to value for the money. Even the open-ended comments on Q10 are decent. Given my low expectations, I feel pretty good about the outcome.

In our business lives, this time of year tends to be the most stressful. Many have their eyes set on June reviews followed by APEC/PEC.[21] It is a natural stressor, and I've been through it many times. With the benefit of hindsight, my request would be that you not let it take over your life. Don't apply the Samratism too literally—you should absolutely have a fair expectation of being rewarded for what you've contributed. But I can confidently say that in 5 years you won't remember what happened in the June 2020 review cycle. I periodically get asked questions like "When did you become principal?" or "When did you open the San Diego office?" And I have to do a lot of calculations in my head to arrive at the answer: "Ummm, I think I made principal a year after my daughter was born, so I guess 13 years" and "Uh, I remember opening the San Diego office the same year my daughter started kindergarten and I could see her playground from my office—so 9 years." If you ask me when I got promoted to manager, consultant, etc., then I have no clue. The firm's system is very fair—so set realistic expectations and let the system take care of the rest.

---

[20] Of course you can't see the green in a black-and-white book, so you'll have to use your imagination.

[21] APEC/PEC = Associate Principal Election Committee/Principal Election Committee. Most privately held consulting firms use a committee like this one to evaluate leadership candidates and "elect" who should move from manager to associate principal and from associate principal to principal. (Did I mention consultants like acronyms?)

■ **Why make your bed every morning if you are going to get back in it at night anyway?** From age 17 to 25 this Samratism saved me at least 5 minutes a day. Prior to that my mother (copied above) harassed me to tidy up. Post that period things got even worse. With my wife, it is not just about making the bed. I get scolded for leaving the medicine cabinet open. Why close it when I have to open it every morning and evening? I always argued. And it is on my side of the bathroom, so why should anyone else care? I also have a perfect pattern by which I arrange my shaving materials, my toothbrush, the toothpaste, mouthwash, hand soap, etc., around my sink. I can enter the bathroom in the middle of the night, not turn on the light, and brush and shave perfectly. But every couple of weeks things just disappear into cabinets and drawers, requiring me to start the process all over again.

I have applied this Samratism to my professional life as well. Consultants are perfectionists by nature. We often want everything to be fully buttoned up before showing it to a manager or the client. I find the opposite to be more effective. Many times it is better to involve others in the process early. Show them a half-developed product, get feedback, and build. It is especially important nowadays where the business situation changes by the day. So it is better to show a client a half-made product first, make necessary course corrections and then proceed to finish it off.

As we head into Mother's Day weekend, I want to wish all the mothers in this group and the few that are about to be moms a very Happy Mother's Day. People always say things like "My mother is the best in the world." Not to bring up statistics again, but that is just statistically impossible. I will say though that my mother is the best one I could have asked for and my wife is the best one my daughter could have wished for. And I am sure each of us can convincingly say that about each of our moms. A special thank-you to each of your moms for shaping the special people you are. Many of us will not be able to see our moms in person this weekend, given the travel restrictions. May I suggest you think of the one thing about your mom that makes you smile? In my case, recently my mom described in great detail her recipe to kill the virus: inhale steam at least twice a day and drink only warm water. I shall pass that on to the president. Also, in her characteristic style, she told me how unfortunate it would be to die of the virus, given that it is not really a *cool* disease. So I shall ensure when my time comes, my exit involves getting hit by lightning on the golf course—that should make for one heck of an obituary.

Stay safe and stay healthy. I love being part of your team.

Samrat

P.S. I started these Friday emails as way to communicate with you during an extremely unsettling time. Now things are slowly going back to "normal." Restaurants are opening up around me, Europe is playing soccer, and liquor stores are open in India. So I think it is time to also move these emails gradually back to normal. I'll still write as I think of things that need to be addressed. It won't be every Friday though—could be once every two weeks, once a month, who knows. But never hesitate to reach out to me at any time if I can be of help.

■ ■ ■

Figure 3. Samrat's Cleaning Service customer satisfaction survey

**Customer Satisfaction
Survey Template**

Monday, May 04, 2020

2

Total Responses

Date Created: Saturday, May 02, 2020

Complete Responses: 2

Q1: How likely is it that you would recommend this company to a friend or colleague?

Answered: 2   Skipped: 0

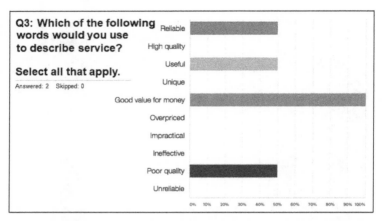

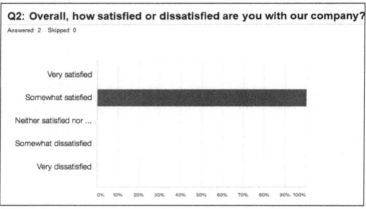

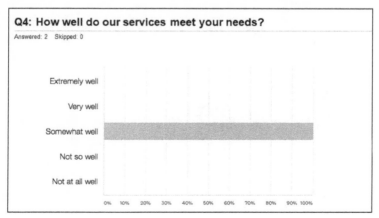

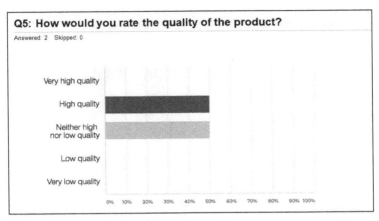

Q5: How would you rate the quality of the product?

Answered: 2   Skipped: 0

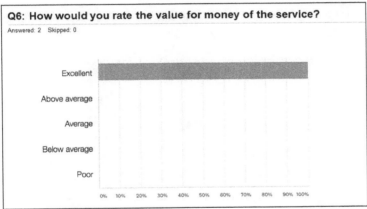

Q6: How would you rate the value for money of the service?

Answered: 2   Skipped: 0

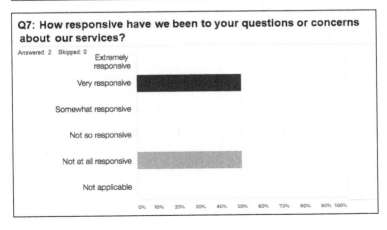

Q7: How responsive have we been to your questions or concerns about our services?

Answered: 2   Skipped: 0

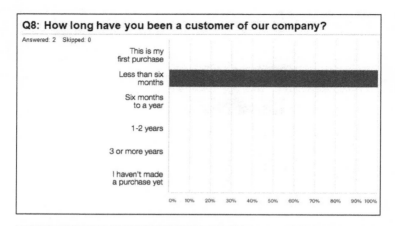

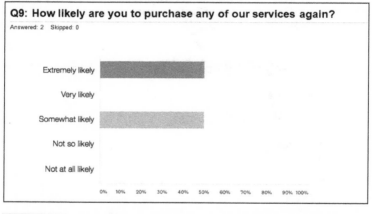

Q10: Do you have any other comments, questions, or concerns?

Answered: 2   Skipped: 0

Respondent 1: There is still some dog hair in my room

Respondent 2: He needs a lot of guidance and tends to skip corners while vacuuming. Doesn't do bathrooms and needs to be told when to clean litter boxes. But since he's free, it's still a great value for the money. And he makes you laugh a lot and never fails to make you smile.

■ ■ ■

AFTER A CERTAIN POINT, senior management communication can get burdensome for both the writer and the reader. I was starting to run out of things to say and began wondering if the younger me would want to be receiving an email from the older me every week. The shock and awe of the immediate crisis was, to a degree, behind us, and people just wanted to get on with their lives. It was time for me to throttle back on the weekly emails and simultaneously find an organizing theme that I could repeat. The concept of "Samratisms" was a natural fit, and over time it was well received by the team. It allowed me to be a bit irreverent, inject humor during a stressful time, and bring the conversation back to business. On Fishbowl there were posts encouraging a book club on "Samratisms"— the early inspiration for this book.

Performance anxiety is felt by every employee of a professional services organization. If asked how they would rate themselves, ninety percent of people in a consulting firm will respond that they perform well above average. And that, of course, is statistically impossible. Yet everyone expects that they will have the fastest path of progression in front of them.

The performance anxiety, however, is not generated only by the individual. Feedback mechanisms in organizations have a large role to play in the problem. A smart employee typically does 70 percent of their job incredibly well, 25 percent at an acceptable level, and maybe 5 percent where it needs improvement. The employee feedback mechanism is the mirror opposite. In any given review session, over two-thirds of the time is spent on telling people what they can do better.

Community pressure is another big issue. Organizations work hard to make people feel like a "family" with team-building exercises, new employee cohorts, cross-globe teams, and the list goes on.

And, just like in a family, trouble erupts when one person appears to jump ahead. There is an extensive amount of human capital spent in managing the drama when two associates who started on the same date get promoted six months apart.

It also seems like some people enjoy disseminating misinformation just to make others more anxious. On the rare occasion I peek at Fishbowl, I see threads where people want to know each other's raise or bonus percentages. Many of the posts feel about right, and then there are those that are just flat-out preposterous lies. The high-ballers set off a chain reaction—those who'd felt they had done well now feel robbed and a nuclear explosion builds.

My hope was that I could give people perspective on the silliness of running after instant gratification. After all, the biggest letdowns come after the biggest initial exhilaration. I have not found the perfect recipe on this topic. It is easy for senior leaders to talk about putting careers in perspective, but the junior folks are intently focused on the here and now. In cases where someone doesn't get promoted, spending a lot of time consoling them can backfire, as it reinforces the story of unfairness they have in their minds. Worse still, it can create an expectation that they will be a shoo-in next time. For better or worse, I have adopted the tack of acknowledging the disappointment and quickly pivoting to poking people to pull up their socks and keep going.

Performance management by accommodation is a road to nowhere.

Of all the emails I sent the team, this one left me with a tinge of regret. Two months into the pandemic, it did look like the virus was being controlled and death tolls would stay low. Hence, towards the end of the email I felt free to take a potshot at the nature of the disease. In the coming months there would be a handful of cases on my team (and for myself) where either family members or close acquaintances became victims of COVID-19. My emails, by design, were meant to be slightly irreverent, but it was a lesson learned that humor regarding health and death is best kept out of the professional realm, especially when dealing with a very large team.

Wednesday, May 20, 2020

To: Compellium Team
From: Samrat Shenbaga
Subject: OBVIOUSISMS TO LENGTHEN
YOUR CAREER IN CONSULTING

Compellium Team:

It feels like a long time since I said it—you fill me with great pride and joy for every moment I get to work with you. We continue to perform exceptionally well as a team and delight clients on a daily basis. Over the past couple of weeks, I've been thinking about a question I am asked often: "How have you survived so long in consulting?" This profession is indeed not for the faint of heart and I have been in it longer than most on this list. Below are a few **Obviousisms** that a consultant must consistently employ to impress clients and co-workers. If said the way Sean Connery would, then the impact doubles, but if communicated how Munnabhai MBBS[22] would, then you can expect 50% loss in effectiveness. I call them "Obviousisms" because you can say them

---

[22] The title character in a 2003 Indian film. He is a gangster who pretends to be a doctor to fool his parents. Cinema at its finest.

about anything in life but when said in a consulting setting, they generate pure magic.

- ■ ***"Take both the short term and long term into consideration."*** I could use this in my personal life as in "In the short term, I should consider the loss of focus in tomorrow's 8 am conference call as I reach for my 3rd Scotch of the night. In the long term, I should figure out whether I will be able to transition to Coors Light from my Bowmore 15 Year once I retire and have a much smaller budget." In consulting, of course, this statement is applied to things like short-term and long-term impact on launch, motivation, product performance, customer perception, sustainability... But you can apply it in seemingly small situations. Let's say the client asks for an adjustment to a forecast model. The answer should be "In the short term, we can incorporate the latest assumptions based on the change in environmental factors. In the long term, who cares? Every forecast by definition is wrong in the long term."

- ■ ***"Assess the needs of all stakeholders."*** In life, I have to do this every Saturday morning when I start vacuuming. First, I must consider if it is past my wife's extended weekend sleeping hours. Next, I must determine if my daughter will be annoyed or pleased if I enter her "office." Then there are the dogs. What if the younger Labrador retriever's feelings are hurt if she thinks I am wasting my time playing with the vacuum instead of throwing the Frisbee for her? And, finally, there is the older Labrador who might be quite inconvenienced when I ask him to move every 90 seconds as he decides to lie down at the exact spot I must go to next. Very simple to apply to our work too. Let's say the client says to you, "Could we change the color on the label heading for Column BQ on the rep sales report from magenta to purple?" A good consultant must never immediately say

"Sure!" The right answer is "Let's see. First, we should think of the rep. What if they are colorblind? Next, we should consider their manager. What if they have an unconscious bias towards colorblind people? Then we have to think of the Microsoft developers. What if they decide to disable purple? So while this may be a good idea in the short term, it could have a long-term negative impact on field morale."

- *"Hadoop."* As CSL of a large account, I get invited to many "steering committees." And many of these involve BT and IT[23] projects. I know as much about BT as Tiger Woods knows about cricket. But given that I am at the table and supposedly a noble firm employee, I have to say something. Typically, by the 20-minute point, my mind starts to drift as people are making important observations like "If we could use 72-bit encryption as we move the metadata from the development environment to the production platform and ensure it only gets slightly wet as it goes through the data lake, then we can reduce the load on the cryptokinetic system." Right when the tech "experts" are getting deeply embroiled in debate, I pipe up, "Have we considered using Hadoop for that?" There is always a big pause as the entire room looks at me. And then without fail someone says, "That is an interesting idea," and off they go again. I have no idea what Hadoop is. But I can tell you nor do the BT and IT people. But they will never admit it. I honestly think it was an April Fools' joke: "**Ha, duped** you!!"

I have a whole bag of tricks, but these are my favorite. Use them and you'll thank me later.

As I wrap up here, I convey with great sadness that one of our dear colleagues lost his father to COVID-19 last week. We get carried away

---

[23] BT = Business Technology and IT = Information Technology. But you knew those, didn't you?

with numbers and curves but are cruelly reminded that there are real people and families behind those numbers. And it hurts even more when it is one of our own. Grief filled me when I heard the news. But I was also filled with pride, as many of you did everything possible to help him in these very difficult times. I wish him and his family the best as they work through their grief.

Take care, stay happy, stay healthy.

Samrat

■ ■ ■

HUMANS STRUGGLE to say "I don't know." Ask any weekend football fan whether the Dallas Cowboys football coach should be fired. It matters not whether said person even knows who the coach is— they are likely to launch into a diatribe on why the poor fellow must go. I am not a football historian, but it does seem like Cowboys fans and opponents alike always want the Dallas Cowboys head coach fired.

The necessity of having an answer to any question is further amplified for subject matter experts. Take Dr. Fauci, for example, one of the lead members of the White House's COVID-19 Response Team. He is clearly very good at what he does and has been able to guide the nation through a major crisis while having to balance competing priorities of the public, his bosses, and scientists. At the outset of the pandemic, when asked about the effectiveness of masks, he had the option of saying "I don't know." For whatever reason, he couldn't bring himself to utter those three simple words. He expressed strongly that masks do not work and then went on to give a long explanation about people moving masks, touching surfaces, and so on. His argument made total sense—until he wanted to change the story three months later. Now, at the time, not having the data, I couldn't have told you whether masks worked or not, but I did know that they couldn't have hurt. And unfortunately, I know that Dr. Fauci's changing position cemented in many Americans' minds the notion that the government was playing games with them.

For a management consultant, it is important to say "I don't know" once in a while—not all the time, as that would just mean the consultant is not worth what they want to be paid. But clients do not expect every consultant to know everything about everything. If there were such a consultant, the whole industry could be scaled down to one person. However, consultants often find it difficult to admit they don't have enough information to have an informed opinion on a given topic.

During the early days of COVID-19, many consultants felt the urgent need to predict the future. While these prognostications were interesting, they often came from people who were a step or two (or an entire ivory tower) removed from the daily work. The nervousness caused by the uncertainty of the business environment led consulting firms to be "provocative" and make exaggerated claims in order to stand out in the crowd. Consultants confidently predicted doom and gloom for the industries they served, which was puzzling and perhaps a bit absurd as that result would put them out of business. Firms had many administrators fretting over daily and weekly forecasts, warning of revenue cliffs, drafting plans for headcount reductions, and plotting different cost-cutting moves. Six months later the same administrators and consultants were perplexed to find many industries *grew* during the pandemic.

Organizations and individuals would reduce a lot of anxiety if they could just say "I don't know." By admitting some degree of uncertainty, an expert in fact gains credibility with those around them—the audience recognizes that the expert provides definite answers when all the information is available but is willing to wait when information is lacking. And the expert gets some leeway if they must later change their assertion because the underlying information changes. In highly uncertain situations, we must take the most logical steps possible, even if we lack 100 percent confidence. We must do the best we can with the information we have, and then, while taking that deliberate approach, we can start planning for various contingencies.

As an expert, one must have the humility to know that everyone else has a brain too. When an expert confidently gets something wrong, the loss in credibility is difficult to recover from.

Sunday, May 31, 2020

To: Compellium Team
From: Samrat Shenbaga
Subject: WHAT IF SADDAM HAD NOT...

Compellium Team:

Hope you are all doing well. On a recent call, out of the clear blue, the client said, "You know what? You guys are just awesome!" It had nothing to do with the topic at hand and definitely was not directed at me. Countless similar moments fill me with pride and joy as you just continue being your awesome selves. My mind wanders a lot nowadays as there is a lot of empty time—and I think that's a good thing. Last weekend I was exchanging texts with a good friend as I wished him Happy Eid. We've known each other for nearly 20 years and have chatted about everything about our lives. But somehow for the first time I mentioned to him that I spent a year in Iraq in the early 1980s. Before anyone calls the CIA on me, let me explain the circumstances...

Back then India and Iraq were pretty good pals. So was the United States—just Google "Rumsfeld shaking hands Saddam." India would send over professors to teach in Iraqi universities, and my father accepted a yearlong assignment. Our tall apartment building in Baghdad sat right on the Tigris across from Saddam's main palace. Anti-aircraft guns were placed on the terrace of our building to protect Saddam from any Iranian Air Force invasion. My younger brother, my mom, and I would go to the terrace to visit with these young soldiers who sat on these guns all day long and longed to see some human life. They were happy to let my 5-year-old brother sit in the seat of their anti-aircraft gun and have some fun. My memory is a bit hazy, but I suspect my mom brought along some Indian snacks for them.

Anyway, the conversation with my friend got to "What if Saddam had never invaded Kuwait?" I shall not get into that as politics and work should not mix. But you can just imagine the possibilities of how the last 30 years of world history would have shaken out differently (and largely for the better). That got me thinking of the choices I've made in my professional life and what if I hadn't made them. I put on my optimistic lens to think of the great things I would have missed out on. For your boredom, I share the top three.

What if I had never joined this firm? Simple answer: my daughter would not exist, at least not in her current form. Like a few other staffers, I met my wife through the firm. I was good friends with another associate, Kaori, in the Princeton office, who had two interesting connections. She was roommates at Yale with our very own Jen, and they joined the firm at the same time. And she was childhood friends with my now-wife when they spent months on the road in skating competitions. One evening Kaori invited a bunch of us to the famous Triumph Brewery in Princeton. My now-wife was new to the area in her job as a math teacher at Montgomery High and was part of the group. The rest, of course, is history. And now I frequently seek feedback through SurveyMonkey surveys from the two most important people in my life, who I know because of my decision to join this firm.[24]

---

[24] My vacuuming skills have not improved.

What if I had never opened the San Diego office? Professionally, the opening of an office gave me the closest feeling to "entrepreneur" I have had to date. At a personal level, I take joy in knowing that at least one firm couple got created in the office. And it is okay to assume that there will likely be a firm baby at some point as a result. Many firm staffers were able to make their Southern California dream come true because of the office. I don't claim that someone else wouldn't have come along and opened the office anyway; I happened to be the lucky one. And while it would be nice if in 5 years someone says "That Samrat guy did some great client work in San Diego," I will be a lot more thrilled if someone thought "If this guy hadn't opened this office, it is possible I would have never been in San Diego and not had all these friends/family that now surround me" or something like that.

What if I had declined the offer to become Compellium CSL? Short answer: I would not be such a highly appreciated guest of the Marriott. Nor would I be able to thumb my nose at others as I flashed my "boarding group 1" pass to all the other miserable passengers waiting to board an American Airlines flight (the stress created waiting for an upgrade can be a topic of an entire email). Most importantly though (and it is no secret), if I had not joined the Compellium team then I would have missed the wonderful opportunity to be with all of you. It has been such a fulfilling journey as I work with people who think of the collective interest rather than their individual need. Every week someone comes up with a new idea that is amazing. Even more often, there are stories of team members helping each other in unique ways. We can get carried away sometimes measuring revenues, margins, utilization... I doubt in 2035 I will remember the Compellium revenues in 2020. But I already have a long library of fond memories seared into my brain on how we've all been together as a team.

In conclusion, there is no big "aha" here. Perhaps if someone is feeling down, they can use their reflection time to think of all the positives that have come from decisions they've made in their life. It is easy to get bogged down in the negativity of "If I hadn't made this choice, I would not have to deal with xyz." I found it more fun to think of "If I hadn't done xyz, then here is the cool thing I would have missed out on." Take care and stay healthy. As always, let me know if I can help.

Samrat

■ ■ ■

BUSINESS LEADERS often ponder their legacy. They obsess over which strategic changes they made will be remembered by future generations. How will history judge them? When someone looks at the headquarters building in twenty years, will they say "This is all possible because of what Bill did two decades ago"?

Politicians and public servants are even more self-centered. They wonder how they will be portrayed in history books. Will a street be named after them? Could it be a highway? Even better, an airport? There is a reason why "US Presidents" frequently shows up as a category in *Jeopardy*. Other than contestants who memorize gigabytes of trivia, most Americans have no idea what each president influenced. When Alex Trebek[25] reveals an answer, 10 percent of the audience thinks, "That guy was a president?" And over three-fourths of the audience mutters in exasperation, "How am I supposed to know that JFK signed the Equal Pay Act?" The harsh reality is that no one remembers a legacy other than the person themselves, their nearest family, and a whole bunch of trivia buffs looking to pick up a few bucks on *Jeopardy*.

In business, by the time one is ready to retire from a firm, their value (unbeknownst only to them) has already been diminishing for many years. People whisper behind the person's back things like

---

[25] Sadly, Alex Trebek died after I wrote this. RIP, Mr. Trebek. The show won't be the same without you.

"Why is he even here?" or "Why does she keep saying the same thing at every meeting?" or "It is nice to hear his fifteen-year-old story, but that approach just wouldn't work today."

For a business leader, it is safe to assume that once the farewell party is thrown and the generic email about their amazing accomplishments is issued, everyone in the firm will forget about them in a month. There are exceptions to the rule: Jobs, Gates, Rockefeller. But I bet you the naming rights to the future Shenbaga Orlando Airport that more than half the employees at any US company cannot name their company's previous CEO. On average, consulting firms grow 15 percent a year while experiencing 15 to 20 percent turnover. So anywhere from a fourth to a third of employees are in their first eighteen months at the firm. They have little interest in knowing about the "trailblazers" who shaped the company decades ago.

What good leaders are remembered for are small pieces of advice, little gestures that show they care, and simply being good human beings. Every time I get frustrated with a nonsensical assignment, I remember the counsel a senior partner gave me at a time when I was particularly agitated: "Hey, I know that sometimes work feels like it stinks. But remember that others go through much more pain and get paid much less than you do." After an especially frustrating week another partner advised, "Don't get consumed by short-term setbacks. There are many people in your orbit who benefit from your efforts—like your family and your team." Those simple pieces of advice have guided multiple career choices I have made and dilemmas I have overcome.

The more one fantasizes about how different the world would have been had it not been for them, the sooner they get forgotten. Living in the moment and being present for your teams is the way to go.

Friday, June 12, 2020

To: Compellium Team
From: Samrat Shenbaga
Subject: MORE GUIDELINES FOR LIFE &
WORK—USE WITH EVEN MORE CAUTION

Compellium Team:

Time is flying by and it is over 3 months since we entered this new state. The one constant for me is the pride and joy I feel every day for being part of this team. An email would not suffice to summarize the list of things that make you awesome, so you will just have to take my word for it. A few weeks ago I wrote to you about a couple of "Samratisms" I follow (inspired by the insipid movie *Samrat & Co.*). For your consideration, I present a couple more:

- ***The long term is but a sum total of multiple short terms.***
  In my final year at IIT Kharagpur,[26] the most vexing question

---

[26] IIT = Indian Institute of Technology. There are multiple campuses today, with Kharagpur being the first one established post-Independence. The IITs are held in high regard as much for the great degree of difficulty in getting admitted as for the quality of education they provide.

posed by recruiters was "Where do you see yourself in 20 years?" In my head, I would say to myself, "That is the dumbest question. I don't know if in 6 hours my friends and I will go off campus to the shady bar that sells even shadier liquor. Or if we will be able to sneak the booze into the dorm and avoid the risk of bicycling while drunk. How the heck do I know about 20 years from now?" But I was well trained and would go off on an eloquent rant: "I aspire to gain real life experience in your welding department, which will then prepare me to learn business, which will in turn help me achieve my father's dream of his son being a startup king." Over time, I have come to the conclusion that overthinking beyond a 6-month window is futile. Case in point is my decision to join the Compellium team two years ago. I was asked on a Friday whether I had any interest in moving my family cross-country and taking on a client that I had no clue about. I could have built a highly sophisticated algorithm that simulated various possibilities and spent 3 weeks pondering short-term and long-term implications. Instead I had a few discussions with my wife and after a few Google searches, I was good to go on Monday. It sounded like a good enough idea for 6 months. And two years out, so far, so good.

My learning is that if I overthink a decision, then I just find reasons to do nothing. If a decision feels right for the foreseeable future, is done for the right reasons, and is pursued with integrity, then what's the harm? As you think about options here at the firm or in your career, don't get caught up in the stressful exercise of predicting every possible outcome in the future. Even if a decision does backfire, there are so many other paths to pursue. Don't get me wrong— one should have broad, long-term goals. But getting fixated on them is unhealthy as we don't control 50%+ of what happens. Forget my recruiting interviews from 25 years ago. All I can say is that even 25 months ago I would not have predicted that I would be part of the most amazing team at this firm.

- ***Inconsistent parenting is the best form of parenting.*** There is an entire industry that publishes books on "what you should expect when expecting." There is also a library of books on best ways to raise your child. 15 years ago my wife bought all such books and read them all. I barely got past page 10 on any. The one concept I found extremely confusing was "consistent parenting." Growing up, I experienced the most inconsistent parenting possible. What my mom said was seldom okay with my dad, and vice versa. And even within each of them there was constant inconsistency. For example, I would periodically joke to my IIT Delhi professor dad that the IITs were only prestigious because the high quality of students they attracted completely masked the poor quality of the faculty. On some occasions this astute observation would be met with healthy laughter and on others with a stinging rebuke. Given that I could never predict my parents' reaction to any issue, I always took the path of best behavior, which was likely to create the least trouble. And while you might disagree, I think I turned out okay. I argued with my wife that if parents are consistent, then the kids will quickly figure out what the boundaries are and manipulate the system to their advantage. If you are inconsistent, the kid never knows where the boundary is and is bound to assume the worst and act their best. As you likely have surmised by now, I was relieved of all parenting duties early on, but I still stand by my argument.

In our business, consistency is important. Clients expect us to consistently deliver high quality and service. No one does it better than this team. At the same time, clients can also get bored with consistency, however exceptional it might be. The best way to keep ourselves and clients excited is to periodically introduce some "inconsistency." Can we surprise a client by asking "We've been doing this the same way for 2 years and it works, but shouldn't we try something different and better?" Or are we bold enough to say, "I am not sure why we are doing this at all. We could be using our collective energies to do something else." I expect that clients will be delighted by this type of "inconsistency" and our creative impulses will go into overdrive. If you are getting bored or comfortable with what you are doing for the client, it is likely a good sign that it is time to inject some inconsistency.

As always, use with extreme caution. The firm takes no responsibility for my views—and nor do any of my blood relatives. If there is anything I can do for you, just ask. Stay healthy and take care.

Samrat

■ ■ ■

ORGANIZATIONS EXPEND a significant amount of energy in defining their long-term vision and strategy. Every couple of years a company declares that it needs to "innovate" (variants include "be bold," "move to the next generation," or "create a new tomorrow"). Think tanks are convened, external benchmarking is initiated, buzzwords are identified, and fancy slides are built with "We will be here in three years, five years, ten years." After many weeks, glossy posters are put up in the cafeteria, rollout sessions are run with big groups, and words like "impact," "innovation," and "reinvent" make it onto every slide.

The obvious fact ignored in these exercises is that a good chunk of people building this grandiose vision will not be around (at least not in their current position) when the organization gets to its post-card destination. Most of the task force members and executives have pending personal milestones on their mind—retirement, kids' weddings, grandkids. And there is little incentive for a frontline manager to turn their small department upside down now for a strategy that won't take place until five years from now; there are too many immediate issues to address and goals to meet.

It is important for organizations to define a long-term vision and strategy, but spending too much time defining all the details of how to get there leads to wasted human capital. The conditions both within an organization and in the external environment are ever evolving. A detailed plan built for five years out is likely to become obsolete within a year.

Hence, I advocate for near- to medium-term focus. Many call this type of approach "narrow-minded" or "unambitious." I would not disagree. However, I can guarantee that this approach aligns much better with human behavior, which needs to observe the reaction to every action. Teams are much more likely to make *some* progress as opposed to *no* progress.

As a medium-term thinker, I often find that a person who claims to be a long-term thinker is one who either has no idea what they are talking about or one who knows they will not be around in the "long term" to have any accountability for the outcomes. If a basketball coach says, "We are building this program for the long term," it is just code for "Don't expect any victories for the next few seasons; I just need to collect this massive paycheck for the next five years before I can retire happily."

Practical leaders focus on what they can see and rally their troops to go get it.

Friday, June 26, 2020

To: Compellium Team
From: Samrat Shenbaga
Subject: WHAT HAPPENED TO AI?

Compellium Team:

The first half of 2020 is almost in the history books. From a business performance standpoint, this team continues to hit it out of the park. But the financial figures pale in comparison to the pride and joy you fill me with every day with stories of your dedication to clients, care for each other, and resiliency in the face of various challenges. Hats off to you. Congratulations to those who were promoted this cycle. Good news—you got promoted. ☺ Bad news—we are going to work you harder now. ☹ Equally important, for the handful who might be disappointed that they have to wait longer, know that you are just as special. This moment is but a blip in your career and there are many successes awaiting you.

As might be evident by now, my mind often wanders aimlessly. So this email is a "rambler"—no real point to it other than that my wandering mind needs to put something down on paper. A few days ago, I was wondering what happened to all the buzz around AI.[27] Prior to the virus, AI was everywhere. Not a week passed by without an AI webinar. There was an unwritten rule that any presentation must mention AI at least a dozen times. The topic didn't matter—we were going to use AI for call plans, goal setting, forecasting, adding and subtracting numbers, making sense of what the heck a CSL was rambling about... AI was going to replace doctors, consultants, pilots, chefs, janitors... But the virus came and AI appears to have gone underground. I admit I am an AI hoopla skeptic—it can be powerful, but we must separate the reality from the hype. However, I believe there are many problems AI could solve to improve our professional lives. Here are my suggestions for AI:

- **Ensure the writer really wants to hit the "Reply All" button.** To begin with, this feature should never have been created. But given that it exists, a smart algorithm should figure out:
  - ◻ Given the type of reply the person has drafted, is it really a good idea to send back to a broad group of colleagues/friends/family?
  - ◻ Will this one reply-all set off a chain of reply-alls that is going to be painful for everyone to delete?
  - ◻ Was the email originator really even looking for a reply? Some reply-alls can cause significant embarrassment. During my younger days, a departing associate sent a farewell email to the office with all the requisite clichés: "You are the best ever, it is all about the people, I have learnt so much, look me up." Unfortunately, one of his friends hit reply all and as a consequence informed the entire office how the departing person really felt about his experience. Oops! (P.S. I do like the e-storm[28] reply-alls a lot.)

---

[27] AI = Artificial Intelligence.

[28] E-storms are when the writer explicitly declares that they want to invite a ton of ideas through mass emails. They take on the responsibility of monitoring and synthesizing the responses.

- **Inform the speaker that they are double muted.**[29] A common occurrence on Zoom calls is when someone's lips are moving but they can't be heard. Multiple people tell the speaker they have to unmute. Speaker takes action but still only lips are moving. After further prodding, the speaker comes in with a sheepish "Sorry, I had double muted myself." Admittedly this issue has gone down since we did away with the "call me" feature (don't get me started on that one). But there are still valiant souls who dial the 4 long numbers required to use their phone—all in the pursuit of the safety of double muting.

- **Develop a recommendation rating for whether one should attend a meeting.** I have mentioned before that I get invited to a lot of meetings. There has to be an AI algorithm that can combine the number of invitees, time of meeting relative to my tee time, my height compared to others on the invite list, etc., etc., to give me a recommendation. In the office days, there was a ton of incentive to attend large meetings, especially if they were held during lunch hour and as an office forum. I would hide in the back row during a lunch and learn on "advanced data sorting techniques using AI" while munching on the free sandwiches and chips, and let my mind wander aimlessly. But now I have to bring my own beer, chips, and salsa to the Friday Forum while sitting in a Zoom call—where is the fun in that?

- **Automatically delete emails based on past readership patterns.** Just imagine how nice it would be if an AI algorithm had deleted this email before you wasted 3 minutes of your life reading it. There are many emails that I don't open just based on the subject line. A classic example is the litany of time entry reminders. Twice a month, I get about 6

---

[29] You hit the Zoom mute button. And then for good measure you hit the mute button on your headset or phone as well. Belts and suspenders.

reminders in different forms (directly to me, CSL reports, OMP[30] funny email, etc.). I've been at this firm for more than 21 years. For all those years, time entry has been due on the 15th and 28th/29th/30th/31st (I used to get paid on the same dates too but that changed for some random reason—don't get me started on that either), and I have an impeccable time entry record. A number of wild emails aren't going to teach this old dog new tricks. And clearly many people here don't pay attention to these emails either—the Compellium team has the dubious distinction of the worst time entry discipline across all CSTs. ☹

Perhaps ADS[31] champions on the team will take my humble suggestions into consideration. That's the end of my ramble. Stay safe, stay healthy, and rest up. If I can do anything, let me know (and I will refer you to AI).

Samrat

■ ■ ■

THERE IS NO DOUBT that science and technology have transformed the way humans run their lives. However, transformational change takes decades and sometimes centuries. For their own survival, consultants must fill the intermediate time period with hype. And once in a while we are brought to the stark realization that science hasn't really progressed all that much.

Take the whole COVID-19 situation as an example. The medical community has made tremendous progress in tackling potentially deadly conditions such as cancer, stroke, and heart disease, but was stumped by the most traditional of problems, a respiratory

---

[30] OMP = Office Managing Principal.
[31] ADS = Advanced Data Science.

virus. We all had to resort to tactics used during the 1918 influenza pandemic: don't breathe on each other, wear a physical barrier over your nose and mouth, stand far apart, and wash your hands. The COVID-19 vaccine did arrive but not before one of the deadliest pandemics in human history had lapped the world.

In the same vein, the case of the missing Malaysian Airlines Flight 370 still gives me sleepless nights. We have thousands of satellites in space, GPS systems, drones . . . but we have not been able to locate one of the largest passenger jets for seven years. Nature has a way of humbling technological progress.

In consulting, I find that a new life-changing concept is announced every two years. "Big data" was a big deal. When it became a thing, I wondered whether it was data in a big font. Or perhaps data that required big brains? Every consulting firm had an informal rule that any slide must have at least two references to big data. No one was going to disagree if you said, "The top line of your business will jump dramatically by exploiting big data." It sounded even more impressive to say, "Big data adds agility to your decision-making and can meet your customer needs in record time." I sat in many meetings where the entire audience nodded in agreement.

One day I leaned over to the person next to me and asked him what exactly big data was. He first gave me a look that said "Seriously, you don't know?" When pressed he mumbled, "It is big data, you know," and quickly exited for a bathroom break. Eventually a no-BS colleague explained to me that big data was nothing but lots and lots of data—something we had had for many years.

My philosophy is to ask questions, and when the answers feel vague, ask more questions. Typically, any time someone tells you that the latest trend will solve all humankind's problems, it is time to get them to peel the onion. More often than not you are likely to find a logical but not magical answer.

It is important for consultants to know the reality of what they are pitching to clients. Trust is built over many years in a consultant-to-client relationship. If the client ends up peeling the onion and finds a stinky garlic, the consultant will soon be shown the exit. Innovation and disruption are the key to success in the consulting business, but adding a dose of humility and realism is the key to longevity.

Friday, July 24, 2020

To: Compellium Team
From: Samrat Shenbaga
Subject: MAXIMIZING THE UTILITY FUNCTION

Compellium Team:

We continue to roll through the summer months, and I hope you are finding small ways of safely enjoying yourself. Your accomplishments continue to fill me with great pride and joy every day. You have demonstrated to Compellium during the past 4 months that our consultants are true partners that they can count on. There are many stories of selflessness, dedication, and flexibility that our staff have displayed to help their Compellium counterparts navigate critical situations.

In the last 3-4 weeks, I have hit some key milestones both professionally and personally. On the personal front, I moved to what many call "the wrong side of the 40s." I am at the age where I keep telling myself I feel young, but I also recall that when I was 21, I used to think of this age as the beginning of the end. My daughter is a high schooler (albeit a virtual one to start with). Those two events put together start raising the question of "What am I going to do with my life 4 years from now?" As the big responsibilities such as raising a kid are knocked out, one has to at least start thinking of what the next phase of life could look like. On the professional front, I have completed 2 years of being part of the Compellium team. While that is still relatively new, time flies when one is having fun. Before I realize it, it will be 4 years. So it is a good time for introspection to ensure I am making the right contributions to the team and that I am confident I will still be enjoying myself.

Over 4 years ago, someone in the San Diego office asked me, "Why have you stayed at the firm so long?" I reshaped the question to "Why am I at the firm?" In order to answer the question, I did what comes naturally to me—I created a formula. When I was pondering my recent milestones, I decided it was time to revisit the formula and update it. I have attached my old and new.

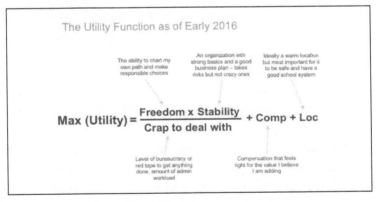

The Utility Function as of Early 2016

The ability to chart my own path and make responsible choices

An organization with strong basics and a good business plan – takes risks but not crazy ones

Ideally a warm location but most important for it to be safe and have a good school system

$$\text{Max (Utility)} = \frac{\text{Freedom x Stability}}{\text{Crap to deal with}} + \text{Comp} + \text{Loc}$$

Level of bureaucracy or red tape to get anything done, amount of admin workload

Compensation that feels right for the value I believe I am adding

Figure 4. My utility function as of early 2016

The core idea is that each one of us enjoys what we do for a variety of different reasons. At any given time, there is a particular utility function that we are trying to maximize. In my utility function, the multiplicative factors are the biggest drivers. The denominator captures all the non-ideal stuff everything in life entails. But if the denominator gets too big then it can destroy the utility function. The additive factors are important, but by themselves cannot compensate for any downfalls created by the first part of the equation. So the first part of the equation is the important stuff and the additive elements are the cherry on top.

The thing about the utility function is that it is ever evolving. For example, compensation and location were multiplicative factors for me early in my career but have been altered and lowered in weight now. I was greatly energized when I built my new utility function over the weekend (see below) and will continue to look for ways to maximize it.

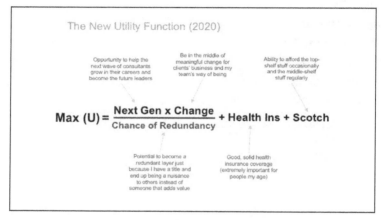

Figure 5. My utility function as of 2020

The function is especially a good help on days when I am feeling really ticked off about something with work ("Why did I ever take this on?" or "Aren't there better things I can be doing in life?"). During those times, the utility function gives me fair balance and helps make a rational decision. It has guided me in making informed decisions on role/space/career changes and prevented me from just going with the "grass is greener on the other side" theory.

Build your own utility function if you fancy, and if you do, I sure would like to see it! Take care, stay safe, and stay healthy. As always, do not hesitate to reach out if I can be of help.

Samrat

■ ■ ■

I HAVE OFTEN BEEN TOLD that one should be passionate about their job. Professional development coaches will use phrases like "you only live once" or "follow your dreams." But is it really that simple? Is anyone ever really "all in" on whatever they are doing? Doesn't everyone have varying degrees of regret about the profession they are in? Sports stars are often held up as being intensely passionate about their game. The top-paid athletes are portrayed as students of their art who spend every waking hour trying to get better. But I imagine that when LeBron James is playing a prime-time game on Christmas day, even he has a small amount of regret about not having a regular job that would give him the day off to be with his family.

Many of us put up with our jobs. Some of us like our jobs. And a few of us love our jobs. But a job or career fits within the broader scheme of life. In my line of work, unpredictability in work hours is an expectation, as clients' needs are not always set in stone. If they have an emergency, we must react. In the aggregate, the overall number of hours may be only slightly higher than comparable professions; however, consultants are paid a premium for their expertise and willingness to upend their lives at a moment's notice. When I interview candidates and ask them why they want to be in consulting, they always say, "I know the hours are unpredictable, but I thrive in that exciting environment" or "Consulting gives me an opportunity to travel, and I like to see places." However, once hired, every employee wants to know how they can manage their work-life balance. If assigned a project that requires them to travel two or three nights a week, they provide excuses for why they can't be gone for more than one night a month ("I have an elderly cat that needs constant attention"). Those who are willing to travel quickly become deflated when they end up in places like

Paris, Ohio, rather than Paris, France. And after eighteen months at the firm, the now-seasoned consultant will make observations about how competing firms have a much better model for their employees. It is inevitable that the grass is greener on the other side—but it is still just grass.

Everyone should get used to the fact that there is no such thing as a perfect job. In consulting lingo, there are pros and cons to every situation. The only question is whether the pros adequately outweigh the cons. If they don't, then get off your behind and do something about it—the world is full of opportunities!

Friday, August 1, 2020

To: Compellium Team
From: Samrat Shenbaga
Subject: LEARNING FROM MACHINES—
NOT THE SAME AS MACHINE LEARNING

Compellium Team:

We have another month under our belts—how time flies. As we continue to sail through the days, weeks, and months, the pride and joy I feel for being part of your team multiplies. Even as the pandemic continues to be volatile, your poise and composure under pressure never ceases to amaze. Over the months many of you have also sent me very heartwarming responses which keep my spirits up. In the last few days some experiences with clients and projects rekindled for me a couple of "Samratisms" that I live by. They are presented here for your consideration.

- ***Real environmentalists drive gas guzzlers.*** On a good day, my car is able to produce 14 miles per gallon. My wife does even better with her vehicle delivering 12 MPG. There have been occasions when as I was pulling out of the gas station the needle on the gas meter was already coming down. I can almost hear the gasps and feedback in the health-check[32]: "The Compellium CSL is a tree killer!" Just hear me out first. The more fuel inefficient my cars are, the faster the world will run out of gas. The faster we all suck all the oil out of the planet, the quicker we will be forced to switch over to clean and renewable energy. Human nature is such that till there is a crisis, we really don't do anything about the underlying problem. If there is a silver lining to this pandemic, it is that in the future vaccines will be developed within a year. But why did we need a pandemic in the first place to figure that out? It is just human nature—that's why "necessity is the mother of all invention" has been a long-held belief.

Now how does this apply to our professional lives? My advice is that *it should not.* A successful consultant is always re-inventing so that they don't end up in a situation with their backs up against the wall and then they have to pull a rabbit out of the hat. Of course, there are always unforeseen situations and we deploy our creative selves to solve them. But we should commit ourselves to always think two steps ahead. Otherwise, the present status of a project will look great but there is a hidden trap waiting.

- *Always aspire to be a dishwasher (the machine and not the person).* Growing up in India I didn't have a dishwasher. Heck, the best I had was 4 hours of running water a day—and for half that time there wasn't enough "pressure" for the water to get to the second floor. My first residence in the US that I shared with 4 other grad students (2004 15th Street, Troy, NY) barely had stable ceilings, so forget a

---

[32] Annual employee satisfaction survey.

dishwasher. My first dishwasher came with my 1-bedroom apartment in Fox Run Apartments in the wildly exciting town of Plainsboro, NJ. I had no use for it till I discovered that I could store my whiskey bottles in it. The first time I used a dishwasher was on the second serious date with my now-wife. On the first date she had me take out the trash from her apartment. I guess I passed that test, so on the second date she asked me to load her dishwasher. After some creative rearrangement, I got the dishes in pretty good. I asked where and how I put the soap in. She came over to inspect my work, and exclaimed, "These dishes haven't been rinsed! They have food crumbs all over them. And you have to handwash some of these dishes as they can't go in a dishwasher." I was quite puzzled. If I have to scrub the dishes with all my might before I load them into the machine, what good is it anyway? It is not a dish**washer**; it is just a dish**sanitizer**. And who invents a machine which can't accommodate half of the potential candidate pool?[33] To this day, it is an active debate in my household. The dishwasher always wins and now there are two dishwashers in the kitchen, both of which see active use.

The dishwasher taught me an important lesson in consulting. While as consultants we are the experts at arriving at a solution, the client is the one who eventually owns it. So we need to get them to have equal ownership throughout any project. Many times they have to do work to make the project successful. Now, we are nice people, and often we don't want to bother the client. When that temptation creeps up, we should ask ourselves if we are really helping

---

[33] Or is it just my wife who buys a whole lot of stuff that can't go in the dishwasher—cast iron, nonstick pans, crock pots, etc.?

the client in the long run if we just take on their responsi-bilities. At Compellium a lot of what we do requires active involvement from the client. Let's always be in the mind-set that we are working **with our clients as opposed to *for* them**.

As always, use with extreme caution. A quick word on business. For many of us, COVID-19 is becoming more personal as acquaintances, family, friends become infected. I recognize this introduces an extra level of stress and we can expect the coming months will have ups and downs. As a Compellium PAM team we have committed to "responsible BD." We want to ensure that we are pursuing the right opportunities with Compellium to keep the entire team appropriately busy. But we also don't want to chase business just for the sake of it and create more stress. It is a delicate balance, and we'll continue to keep a close eye on it. As always, if I can help in any way, please do not hesitate to reach out. Take care and stay healthy.

Samrat

■ ■ ■

IT IS WELL DOCUMENTED in business and behavioral research that positive reinforcement motivates people up to a certain point. But fear is what really gets people to hustle. Humans are far more afraid of what they stand to lose. Let's say I told you that you could add a nice gazebo to your house if you worked an extra five hours a week. It is a nice aspiration, and you will start working harder, but if other obligations get in the way, you won't be disappointed to lose out on the gazebo. Now what if I told you that if you didn't work at least two hours more a week I would take a hammer to your sports car? I bet you would log in at least five more hours a week just to make sure you didn't fall below that dreaded threshold.

I am often reminded of a tale one of our founders told the partner group to help them realize that they needed to always be afraid. He spoke of lions and gazelles and how "somewhere in Africa this morning a gazelle is waking up knowing that it has to outrun the fastest lion or it will be lunch." As the partner group weighed the gravity of the situation for the gazelle, one of the younger partners piped up, "But doesn't the gazelle just need to run faster than the slowest gazelle?" In either case, fear is what keeps the gazelle going.

In a team environment, it would be a disaster for a team leader to always rule by fear. While it could work for a short period of time, the power of the collective team is much greater than that of the leader. However, there is also an undue amount of attention paid to "motivating" employees. Treating people well, acknowledging their successes, rewarding exemplary behavior is one thing. Coddling them and protecting them from any bad news is another. On the contrary, shielding employees from any negative feedback or consequences has a detrimental impact on their progression. And when the going gets tough, as it inevitably will, the corporate pendulum swings to the opposite side—from motivating to fearmongering—leaving many young employees perplexed.

The occasional gentle reminder to everyone about potential negative outcomes is helpful. People deserve to know that if they want to have meeting-free Fridays then business might eventually suffer, which will affect their raises (or even the employment status for a subset of them). A first-year consultant from an elite university might need a reminder that his college degree is what got him the job but won't earn him a raise if his current ineptitude continues. The proverbial gentle kick in the rear is about as useful a managerial trick as has been invented.

Tuesday, September 1, 2020

To: Compellium Team
From: Samrat Shenbaga
Subject: THE AUGUST SUMMARY

Compellium Team:

Fall is slowly approaching, and August definitely went by at warp speed. Regardless of what speed we go at, the one constant is the pride and joy you bring for me through all kinds of remarkable things you do. The macro environment continues to be volatile—but your resolve and steadfast focus never cease to amaze. Not a week goes by without another incredible client or team story getting added to my email folders.

August came with many personal milestones for me. **August 10th** marked the 20th anniversary of getting married in front of a judge in the wonderful courthouse of Plainsboro, NJ. One of the witnesses was a firm staffer. Back then we had assigned seating in the office. I left nonchalantly for the courthouse during my lunch break, and when I returned my officemate asked, "Is there something you need to tell me?" Didn't seem like such a big deal to me, but my officemate refused to speak to me for a week. The courthouse wedding was followed up with receptions in Madras (Chennai now) and New York City, leading to different interpretations of my wedding date between my parents and my in-laws. By this point you would realize that I tease my wife constantly. So after 20 years of marriage, she was unfazed when I asked my mother-in-law if the return policy was still valid!

The following day marked the 4-year birthday of my highly energetic black Labrador, Chloe. She got extra Frisbee treatment as a gift.

August 15th is an all-encompassing date in my life. It is famously India's Independence Day. In 1996, it was the date when I moved to the United States. I recall having about $150 in US currency and another 120 deutsche marks, both of which my father had scrounged during his international trips. Nowadays whenever there is a big purchase in my household, I grumble to my wife that I had more money in my checking account back then than I do today. August 15th also turned out to be the birthday of my senior dog, Riley, now an 8-year-old yellow Labrador. His brain is still as wild as it always was, but his walks are getting shorter. He's been with me through many major events in life—to the point that I have at least two permanent marks on my body from injuries I incurred chasing him. And lastly, to make things easier a cousin of mine decided to have his wedding on August 15th this year. It was my first experience with a Zoom wedding. It was good to see that everyone wore masks other than the bride and groom.

And just as August wraps up, it is exciting to see our leadership ranks grow. ***Congratulations to Pranav, Scott, and Arrvind, who spend the majority of their time on Compellium, on their elections to AP/P!***[34] ***Joining them are Liz, Tim, Joe, Reena, Abhinav, and Matt, who are/ have been active SMEs on the account.*** (And sorry if I missed someone.) There are many unique things about each of them that you've either experienced or will hear about in upcoming forums. The one

---

[34] Are you keeping up with the acronyms? Recall P = Principal and AP = Associate Principal.

common thread is their passion to keep getting better. Every time I talk to them, they are looking for a better way to solve a client problem, presenting an idea on creating a better experience for the team, wondering if we are missing something. Their passion and drive make them and everyone around them better. I certainly hope they will pause to savor the moment. And the even more exciting part is that we have more leaders that will grow on this team and every year this team will have a bigger representation on the AP/P list. With the increasing diversity of work we do at Compellium, I certainly hope everyone in this group will find growth opportunities.

Our business performance continues to be strong in 2020. I expect that this year will be the most successful one yet for the Compellium-firm relationship. This feat is impressive in itself, and doing it in the background of COVID-19 makes it a bit surreal. I recognize that COVID/Zoom/WFH fatigue is a real thing. Taking vacation may feel futile, but try to take 1-2 days off here and there just to let your mind idle. Last week I spent an entire day in front of the TV and can't really recall what I watched (no, I was not inebriated)—but it felt good.

As always, reach out if I can help. Stay safe and healthy.

Samrat

Figure 6. Riley and me getting a nap

Figure 7. Chloe and Riley playing

■ ■ ■

EXITING AT THE RIGHT TIME is a hard thing to do. We see athletes struggle to come to terms with the fact that their best is well behind them; they must be gently nudged into retirement once it is clear that no one is willing to pay them for nostalgia's sake (perhaps with the sole exception of Kobe Bryant). In the NFL, sports "couples" linger well beyond their utility. As a Green Bay Packers fan, I cannot help but wonder how many more Super Bowl rings Aaron Rodgers would have now if the team had made the logical decision to move on from Mike McCarthy five or six years sooner—it would have been the best for all three parties. Yet they all stuck together in the illogical dream that they could recreate the lucky run they had in 2011. Reid and Mahomes, Lewis and Dalton, Carroll and Wilson, and Tomlin and Roethlisberger all come to mind in the same vein, and in many of these cases the quarterback should be the one to move on, as they are dragging down the coach. The end of the Belichick-Brady era is the closest one can come to perfect separation timing.

Similarly, stocks are a frustrating addiction. Can you think of one time when you heard someone say, "I sold that thing at the exact right time"? But I bet many of us have moaned about how we held on a little too long to a stock that we knew in our hearts could be just past peak.

Business leaders suffer from the same malady. I see three types of leaders in a firm. About 60 percent are truly driving the business. Roughly 30 percent have passed the peak of their personal performance, but their experience and wisdom are invaluable, so even though they might be "overpaid," they play an important part in ensuring the success of the 60 percent. Then there are the remaining 10 percent who are lost; they feel stuck with no place to go. Unfortunately, the 90 percent wonder why the 10 percent are still around. Any given individual need not progress from stage A to B to C. In fact, the 10 percent is a fairly static group. The smart ones in the 30 percent group at some point recognize that their time is up and say their fond goodbyes.

In the professional world, it is important to constantly think about the next step in one's journey. That does not mean that one keeps jumping around. On the contrary, demonstrating success in one's current role is important to being considered for a worthwhile future position. But the "I'm good at this so I'll just keep doing it" mentality will eventually lead to one's getting pushed to an outcome one might not like. In any growing and vibrant firm, there are up-and-comers who will invade their superiors' space in due course. Hence, leaders must look for ways to make themselves redundant in their current roles and find new ones. It is the classic "circle of life" in professional services.

For my part, given my fascination with dates, I start a mental countdown clock as soon as I start a new role. If it is an excruciatingly painful role, then it is my way of telling myself "This thing will be over soon!" But typically, the countdown gives me clear boundaries on how much time I have to deliver the impact I wish to have in the role, when I need to start thinking about succession planning, and at what point I need to know what I will do next. I recognize the mechanism may feel a tad obsessive and could certainly lead to undue pressure if one were to make it the sole focus of one's being.

Over time, I have learned to inject some fun into this self-made game. Recently I took on a leadership position that I determined should last four years. After some brainstorming, I decided to associate my countdown with US presidents. When I got down to forty-five months, it was Trump time; at forty months, it was Reagan. While my execution was not perfect, each month I looked to learn a bit about the associated president. And I was determined that by the time I got to John Quincy Adams, I needed to have a successor in line firing on all cylinders.

Friday, September 18, 2020

To: Compellium Team
From: Samrat Shenbaga
Subject: LIVING AN IMMERSIVE EXPERIENCE

Compellium Team:

We are starting to inch towards the festival/holiday season part of the year. I am sure we will celebrate these events in unique ways this time around. But I get to celebrate every day the pride and joy that I feel for being part of your team. You continue to deliver high quality work and maintain a sense of togetherness despite the lack of physical proximity.

In my 21+ years at the firm, I have exclusively focused on the commercial aspects of pharma. After many years of working on high-powered analytics, I only got a real feel for the work we do after going on a few field rides. It brought to life the realities reps face as they try to get time with a doctor, the broad set of issues different doctors care about, and most importantly how reps use (or ignore) the reports/tools/insights we create for them. So I feel like I have a good feel for the theoretical and practical sides of commercial in pharma. Last year I started getting interested in R&D. The theory is very interesting on drug development, site selection, analytics behind trials, etc., but it was hard for me to get a real visual in my head of what it was all about. I kept desiring an immersive experience. As the COVID-19 vaccine trials kicked off, I decided to add my name to the registry in the US sponsored by the NIH.[35] I had no idea of the chances of being called, but no harm in trying.

Two weeks ago, I got a call from a trial site about 90 minutes away from where I live. They wanted to know if I was interested. First there were a series of questions over the phone to ensure I met the basic criteria. Then I was given an appointment for Friday, September 11, to go in. I won't go through the entire series of events, but a few things stood out.

- **Many people don't really understand how the efficacy of a vaccine is determined.** When informed of my trial participation, both my daughter and father had the same question: "Are they going to spray you with the virus after you get the shot to see if it works?" 😕 I had to explain to them that we were well past the mice part of the experiment.

- **The act of participating in a trial is a bit of a risky proposition.** Since COVID-19 started spiking, I have been following a pretty cautious lifestyle. Everything is delivered to the house. The closest human interaction I have is with people at the golf course, who are usually very far away. Occasionally there is the stop at the gas station, but everyone has masks on. So when I went into the trial site and waited in the reception area with a dozen other people, that was the most "crowded" indoor space I had been in 6 months. I raised my risks of contracting the virus exponentially just by going for the trial.

---

[35] NIH = National Institutes of Health.

- **I don't like shots, but the ancillary tests are way worse.** After all the progress science has made, it still strikes me as odd that I still get poked with needles to extract blood. To make it worse, the technicians always have trouble with me. Some say it is my earthy skin tone; others say my veins don't pop. Regardless, it occasionally leads to multiple pokes. I managed to get through the blood draw fine. Then came the even worse part—the COVID nose swab. I had no idea that they made Q-tips that long and that they could actually go so far up one's nose (now don't make "Samrat has a big nose" jokes). For a second, I was convinced the Q-tip had hit my eyeball. The nurse handed me a tissue to wipe off the uncontrollable flow of tears, which is another risk factor if the tissue had the virus sitting on it.

- **The blinded nature of the trial is not helpful.** As is the norm, they don't tell you whether you are getting the real thing or a placebo (saline water). During my research I read that the placebo is clear and the real thing is darker. When the nurse came over to administer the shot, I sneaked a peek. But alas, the syringe was fully covered with paper with all sorts of serial numbers. The big problem is that without knowing what I got, I won't do full justice to the trial. If they had told me I got the real thing, then I would be running out to restaurants, getting on rides at Disney World, flying to various destinations just for old times' sake. It would be the best way to test whether the vaccine is working. But without knowing I will continue my cautious way of living. Let me chat with my R&D colleagues on whether we can make a convincing argument for unblinded studies.

- **Never before have I eagerly waited for a side effect.** While they don't tell you what you got, one can expect some side effects if you get the real thing. I spent the entire next couple of days imagining soreness in my arm. But that theory went by the wayside when I hit my longest tee shot. Then I kept checking my temperature every hour hoping for a spike. No luck. So either I got the placebo, or this vaccine is really good.

The journey continues when I go back in two weeks for a second shot and then for monitoring visits for as much as 24 months. I have to say that I am really impressed by the care and rigor by which the trials are conducted. But having the real experience of participating in a trial, I am starting to think of many ways they can be made better and faster. I feel good that I can do my small part in speeding up the process of ending this pandemic (my wife also is in the trial). Stay safe and healthy. And as always, let me know if I can be of any assistance.

Samrat

■ ■ ■

DURING THE PANDEMIC, health experts and many in the media used the term "debt of gratitude" to describe what society owed vaccine clinical trial volunteers who were sticking their necks out on untested technologies. While I appreciated the sentiment, I suspected that the emotions of the day combined with the "marketing" needed to get volunteers in quickly was contributing to the fawning over trial participants. However, I knew my motivations, and they were simple:

- A colleague's father and an aunt of mine had passed away from COVID-19, and I felt an urge to do any small part I could.
- I researched the Phase 1 and 2 results and felt good that the vaccine couldn't kill me. And I was worried that if everyone held back, then the vaccines would never arrive. So, speeding up the end of the pandemic was important to me.

- A very minor consideration was the 50 percent chance of receiving the vaccine. That would be a bonus, though it would not really help me in the short term, as the trial was double-blinded and I would not change my pattern of behavior anyway.

Having this clarity of motivation would come in handy a few months later once the vaccines were approved . . .

In the business world, it is essential to know why one is making a decision—what is motivating it? For example, in hiring for an open position, the hiring manager wants a good employee; the candidate wants a good job. Both are starting with motivations in a place of good intent.

But most individuals know there is some amount of marketing that needs to be done to bring people into a company. Job candidates know they are being told the best things about the company. The interviewer knows if they ask the candidate for examples of past performance, the candidate will give three positive examples, not two good and one bad. Neither party is lying, but there is definitely some selectiveness and/or embellishment in the details shared. However, their motivations overlap, and with a bit of luck, the manager-employee relationship will be successful.

The risk, however, is that the initial promises are not followed through on. The candidate doesn't perform at the high level expected; the company doesn't offer the support or bonuses promised. The follow-through needs to be at least 75–80 percent of any promise made initially—whether to a job candidate, customer, or colleague. If those expectations are not met, customers or employees can be lost and antagonists can be created. The short-term gain achieved by overpromising can create long-term pain.

In the case of the vaccine trials, one expected public officials to use some inflated language like "debt of gratitude" in order to recruit volunteers. However, it appears many volunteers were told—via loose promises—that they would be first in line once a vaccine was approved. Others were told that the pharmaceutical company would unblind the study and let people know their status (vaccine or control group) as soon as possible. So when the vaccines received approval and when the "debt of gratitude" turned to criticism of the trial volunteers for attempting to "cut in line," volunteers were rightfully upset. I had gone in with my skeptical eyes wide open so was not surprised by this turn of events.

Everyone involved in the trials might like to position themselves as beneficent (and there is at least a grain of truth in that), but in reality each party had its own motivation. The pharmaceutical manufacturer wanted to get to market as fast as possible. Clinical trial coordinators wanted to enroll as quickly as possible, as their payments are tied to speed and volume of enrollment. The broader population was desperate for a return to some semblance of normalcy; volunteering to get jabbed with a needle would move us closer. Politicians (many of whom contributed to the mess) wanted to keep their jobs; ending the pandemic would help do that. Media outlets wanted their next big storyline; vaccine trial success would provide that.

Luckily, those motivations intersected and led towards a good outcome for society.

For a team or a company to succeed, the individual incentives and motivations must be aligned. The boss must believe the business and earnings can expand. Their direct reports must trust that any pain they put themselves through will lead to a bump in income and to better long-term career prospects. Company management must be convinced that the company would be better off with this team rather than without it. Any time there is misalignment, watch out for the gears to start grinding against each other.

But when promises are broken—when gratitude turns into criticism, when "fair profit" turns into "unbridled greed," when a bear hug turns into a cold shoulder—any goodwill built over the years can disappear in minutes.

Mutual respect in relationships is important regardless of whether they are person-to-person or business-to-person. If either side believes they've been taken for a ride, trust is broken and the affected party will likely never reengage.

Friday, October 2, 2020

To: Compellium Team
From: Samrat Shenbaga
Subject: THE SECOND SHOT

Compellium Team:

Hope you are all well as we enter the final quarter of an eventful 2020. This week a few of us presented the 2021 Compellium plan to the CSC.[36] As I attend these types of forums, the pride and joy I feel in your accomplishments just continues to multiply. You continue to drive remarkable outcomes, lend a helping hand when needed, and maintain poise despite the challenging external environment.

Today I got a second and final dose of the vaccine (or saline water) as part of the clinical trial. The appointment lasted about 2 hours—plus the ~3 hours of commute time. As is often the case, my mind wandered during the 2 hours I sat mostly by myself in the little room. My brain is divided into three parts, and a few of the thoughts that went through them are below.

---

[36] CSC = Client Service Council. This is a rotating group of four principals, including the CEO, who serve as an advisory team to the CSLs.

The logical part

- *How am I supposed to code my timesheet?* It doesn't quite feel like a vacation, especially when I am being poked with needles and having Q-tips that tickle my brain stuck up my nose. It is not sick time, as the goal is to *not* get sick. Could it count as "We Care" time because there is a benefit to society? Or could I think of it as business development for R&D? I shall investigate.

- *What is the personal ROI?* I get paid $150 for each visit. But to start with, the government will take its cut in taxes, so shave off $50. The clinical trial site is ~65 miles away. Just gas for my environment-supporting, gas-guzzling monster is easily $25. Best case, I am left with $75, which makes it a real questionable proposition if I only got the placebo.

- *Do we appreciate healthcare workers enough?* I believe we owe a big debt of gratitude to the various healthcare workers out there. At the site, there are multiple workers who spend all day interacting with volunteers and patients at great risk to themselves. We should be putting these workers right at the front of the line for the vaccine (once approved), and they should never have to pay for a drink at a bar ever again (they should wait till the pandemic is over though).

- *Can't things be even faster?* The only things that needed to be done today were the nose swab and the shot. Both put together took only 5 minutes. But I had to wait around in the room for another 115 minutes. I couldn't help but wonder if we wouldn't be able to shave weeks off the vaccine development timeline if the trial process itself were more efficient. Twice as many participants could have been processed in the same time.

The conspiratorial part

- On the flip side, as I sat around unproductively, I wondered if they might be pumping the virus through the air vents to speed up the vaccine testing process. 😔 I am not making this up—I overheard the investigator tell a person in the next room that the ideal volunteer would be youngsters who are holding COVID parties! Maybe, just maybe, the extended waiting time is part of the trial design.

- If this vaccine really works as well as they claim, why didn't they just give it to the president a few weeks ago? Every TV series I ever watched portrays the US government as knowing a whole lot more than the public. Either those TV shows are lying, or there is something I am not being told. (I do hope the president gets better soon.)

The Fantasyland part

- As my stomach started growling, I wondered if the investigator would accidentally reveal that I got the real thing—and then I could stop for lunch at the Cracker Barrel I saw on my way up. It has been 8 months, which is just way too long to not be able to go to one. I have always believed that there should be a constitutional amendment requiring all Americans to visit a Cracker Barrel at least once a quarter.
- Alternatively, if the investigator were willing to accept a $20 note in exchange for information confirming that I was really inoculated, could I get on a flight to Maui on Wednesday?

Alas, these two remain in Fantasyland.

I shall now spend the weekend hoping for hints of side effects that could confirm administration of the real thing. For those in India, hope you are enjoying your long weekend. Take care and stay safe everyone. The vaccine definitely seems to be chugging along. Patience is the key from here.

Samrat

Figure 8. Vaccine trial site

■ ■ ■

ON DECEMBER 11, 2020, I felt a great sense of personal pride when the first COVID-19 vaccine was approved in the US. After forty-five years on the planet, I felt I had finally contributed meaningfully to humankind. There were twenty-four hours of positivity in the news media, from politicians, from scientists—the whole gamut. And then, from a trial participant's perspective, things got ugly.

As of this writing, Pfizer, Moderna, and J&J are the three authorized COVID-19 vaccines in the US, authorized in that order. Prior to any vaccine's approval, there were two major trial-related questions being debated:

1. When do you "unblind" the trials? That is, when do you let the participants know whether they were in the test group or control (placebo) group?

2. How do you prioritize the clinical trial participants for vaccination after approval?

I touched on the second question earlier. Unfulfilled promises are not useful or ethical. But regardless of what some people were "promised," I had not volunteered in order to gain priority access. As a healthy forty-five-year-old male, I could wait my turn in queue and let frontline workers and people at higher risk go first. I'd waited nine months and could wait another three.

On the first question, however, I had some vigorous disagreement with the "experts." Remember I work in pharma, so even though I'm not a researcher, I do know a thing or two. So let's back up a bit . . .

Drug trials are performed in a "blind" fashion, meaning participants don't know whether they get the drug or a placebo. The test is designed to determine whether there is a statistically significant difference between results in the test group and the control (placebo) group. In other words, the researchers are checking for *efficacy*—does the treatment work? In the COVID-19 case, the vaccines needed to be at least 50 percent effective, and all the candidates blew past that threshold—and that is an amazing testament to the skill and dedication of the scientists who have been laboring away in labs for decades. Additionally, researchers are monitoring *safety*. They want to see zero to minimal safety issues unless an issue can be narrowed to a specific group, e.g., the product can be approved with a warning that it should not be used with people who are pregnant. After safety and efficacy are established, the participants are monitored for a period of time (which could be six months or several years) to continue watching for any long-term safety issues, and in the case of a vaccine, to determine *longevity*—that is, if and when a booster shot will be needed.

Theoretically, the scientists might love to keep the study blind forever (to maintain its purity/just in case), but if efficacy is shown, how long is it ethical to withhold the benefit (the vaccine protection in this case) from the placebo participants? Giving it to them requires "unblinding" the study, but there are minimal guidelines about when to unblind vaccine studies. If a participant drops out of the trial, they are told which group they were in. And in the case of the COVID-19 vaccines, once a vaccine was approved, the researchers were required to unblind anyone eligible for it, such as health care workers, on day one. But beyond that it was up to the pharma companies and the FDA to negotiate the "rules" of their trial. In this case, Pfizer and Moderna took different recommendations to the FDA; however, the FDA advisory boards asked both companies to keep the trials blinded for as long as they possibly could.

The day the Moderna vaccine was approved, Moderna had already lost 25 percent of its trial participants because the Pfizer vaccine had come out the previous week and Moderna had unblinded eligible health care workers. With every passing week, the number of unblinded participants grew as seniors and others became eligible. So in effect, within a month of approval, over half the sample in the trials was unblinded.

At this point—with vaccine efficacy clearly proven and the trial only partially blinded—I began to argue that the trials should be fully unblinded. If tracking long-term effects and the longevity of effectiveness were the goals, the number of people who had been inoculated in the real world far surpassed the number of trial volunteers, thus giving plenty of access to real-world data. (In fact, the pause in distribution of the J&J vaccine didn't result from the findings of clinical trials; it came from real-world results—and its resumption was based on real-world data as well.) The blinded nature of the trials was falling apart and if, as a Moderna senior executive pointed out, they leave a placebo participant out there who dies because they were still in a blind study and didn't have a chance to get an approved vaccine, the guilt would weigh heavy. However, the regulatory authorities didn't appear to agree.

I wrote to experts at the FDA, the CDC, HHS, the White House, and the manufacturer; they never responded. I exchanged emails with the primary expert from a renowned university whose

opinion had guided the FDA to deprioritize clinical trial participants for the vaccine; his explanations for continuing the blind
studies were based on polio trials designed in the 1950s that didn't
take into account real-world data. I spoke with my clinical trial
investigator, who within ninety seconds confirmed my belief that
staying in the trial benefited only his performance metrics, not the
pursuit of better results.

After reviewing the facts, in my mind there was no logical reason for the trial to continue to be blinded and I wanted to know
whether I got the placebo or the real thing. Here is an excerpt from
a comment I posted in response to an article in *JAMA* that debated
the ethics of keeping clinical trial participants in the dark.

> *Similar to another commenter, I am currently enrolled in the
> vaccine trial for one of the approved COVID vaccines. It has
> been a tremendous scientific accomplishment to have two vaccines
> administered to Americans already. The scientists, trial facilita-
> tors, and trial participants must be congratulated on their unbe-
> lievable efforts—this is nothing short of landing on the moon. . . .*
>
> *I am perplexed by the resistance to fully unblind the
> trials. . . . Keeping trials blinded to this point clearly demon-
> strated efficacy. The stated goal of continued blinding is to
> monitor for long-term side effects and longevity of efficacy. I
> have personally corresponded with the experts who recommended
> against unblinding—and I cannot get a straight answer on how
> the study of these effects will be helped by keeping in the dark
> people [who were] injected with saline water. On the contrary, I
> would think it would be better to reset the clock with the placebo
> patients [that is, give them the vaccine] as quickly as possible to
> enable data collection.*
>
> *The other big benefit of unblinding the trial is that 22k vol-
> unteers who received the vaccine can rest easy—not telling them
> is denying them the opportunity to visit an elderly parent in a
> nursing home they have not seen for 9 months. And the last issue*

with keeping the trial blinded is that it removes any incentive for future and current trial participants. By not telling me now which arm I am in, there are two effects: a) a reduction in any moral obligation I feel to continue on the trial, and b) when my turn [to get an approved vaccine] is up, I have to weigh the risks of driving an hour to the clinical trial site versus just hopping over to the local CVS.

Had the study simply been unblinded, I would have gladly stayed in for tracking purposes. Eventually I felt that the best thing to do for my conscience was to drop out of the trial, as it would put my mind at ease and have no negative impact on humankind.

I realize I've gone on about clinical trials a bit long, but here's the takeaway: everyone believes they are an expert on something; some even believe they are an expert on everything. The problem with expertise is that it can be one dimensional. Experts in any field must realize that there are many facets to expertise and that living in their bubble can have unintended consequences.

Whether it's statisticians pumping out papers on the benefits of blinded trials, or ethicists opining on moral hazard and precedent, or business consultants offering their clients advice, deep subject matter experts tend to get immersed in what they do and believe they have the best answers. But much of the time everyone else knows about 80 percent of what the expert knows and can use common sense to fill in many of the gaps.

Experts might assume that everyone else simply doesn't get it, but their theoretical reasons can bump up against logic. When an expert says something, does it pass the sniff test? If they can't answer reasonable questions that push back on what they are saying, that creates suspicion. Things must tie together, or the expert starts losing credibility.

Degrees and credentials alone are not a true measure of expertise. In business the experts who are most respected are ones who surround themselves with people who bring different perspectives and sometimes can be "devil's advocates." Occasionally I will assign a team member the role of pointing out all the holes in my argument or presenting a counterview. I have been surprised how often my "opponent" has caused me to modify the stance I'd built on twenty-plus years of experience and "expertise."

The ability to listen to competing viewpoints, recognize the possibility of more than one right answer, demonstrate a willingness to modify one's position, and blend one's own insights with those of others are the hallmarks of a true expert.

Friday, October 23, 2020

To: Compellium Team
From: Samrat Shenbaga
Subject: LINKING MY DIET TO
2021 BUSINESS PLANNING

Compellium Team:

Hope you are well. While the virus and the related stress ebb and flow around us, we can look forward to the breaks and controlled celebrations that the fast-approaching holidays will bring. My positivity is fueled by the daily sense of pride and joy I feel for being part of your team. The caring, compassion, and collaboration across the team is always on full display.

Over the past couple of months, we have been formulating the 2021 business plan. You'll see highlights in the upcoming town hall. As the CSL, I have the enviable job of being able to participate in brainstorming sessions across the various spaces. As I reflected on common themes for the 2021 plan, a few "Samratisms" hit me. Below are two for your consideration.

- ***Meat eaters should not be required to eat vegetables.***
  When noting down my order, a server often asks, "Do you

have any allergies?" My standard response is "Vegetables, especially if they are uncooked." Don't get me wrong—I do eat vegetables, but only when they don't actually taste like vegetables. I love my matar paneer, vegetable pakoras, baingan bharta.[37] However, you will note that they are either deep-fried or drowned in curry or spiced to the point where it doesn't matter which vegetable is in there. So perhaps Indian cooking techniques are designed to mask the vegetables. I also eat vegetables with my steak as long as they are french fries or onion rings. My wife always asks that I start with a salad. I have argued at length that the act of eating a salad before a steak is hugely duplicative. Salads or the equivalent are what cows eat. Hence by default a salad is already embedded into the steak—so why do I need to eat an extra salad?

How does this even apply to our 2021 plans? Over the years we have streamlined how we deliver work to Compellium. However, there is still room to remove redundancies. Are two people required to check the same output? Can things that require multiple handoffs be automated? Is one team doing an analysis and another team repeating something very similar? A small goal of all this is to improve efficiency. A much bigger goal is to open up time to do newer things. You'll see during the town hall that we have many new frontiers to conquer, and wouldn't it be great to shift time within the team to go after new stuff? After all, when I skip the salad, I always get dessert instead!

---

[37] Matar paneer is a dish with paneer (an Indian cheese) and peas in a spicy tomato-based sauce; pakoras are like fritters (fried, mmm); baingan bharta is a roasted, spiced eggplant dish. And now I'm hungry.

■ *If everyone tells you the book is great, then just wait for the movie.* I have shared my fondness for movies in past emails. On the other hand, I can't remember the last time I read a book. The closest I got was when I pulled out *Tintin in America* from my Tintin collection six months ago, got through 10 pages, and put it back. I find the whole job of reading a book over the course of multiple days fairly impractical. How am I supposed to remember what happened at the beginning when I am getting to the end two weeks later? A movie condenses everything down to 135 minutes, cuts out the fluff, and at the end of it I have the same knowledge of the outcome as I would have if I had read the book. And not to mention, I can knock down a couple of beers and some nachos along the way. I am not saying that books should not exist. But we should treat the movies they are based on with the same respect. Whenever I roll this argument out to my teenage daughter she comments, "You just don't read books because you are not smart enough." I vehemently disagree.

Getting to 2021 plans, we have many ideas that will challenge long-held beliefs and traditions. Sometimes it feels like sacrilege to want to change something that has worked perfectly well for many years. This could have to do with the type of outputs we create or how we do the work. It could also be how we work with the client or with each other or with the rest of the firm. But if we hold on to past things for too long, they have the risk of taking us down. In many cases, we may not replace something old—the goal could be that we have another option, given the evolving preferences of the business and customers.

Well, there you have it. I could have summarized this in a 3-minute video and saved us all a lot of effort. I look forward to seeing many of you at the town hall. Stay safe and healthy (both mentally and physically). Don't hesitate to reach out if I can be of help.

Samrat

■ ■ ■

GOOD ORGANIZATIONS have checks and balances to ensure that one unruly employee does not sink the entire company by taking an action that backfires in explosive ways. In well-run organizations, individuals have a clear understanding of the boundaries they must stay within (which can often be broad) and they have ready access to seasoned professionals who can offer objective advice on how to handle issues that might be out of bounds. This arrangement provides a healthy balance of individual autonomy and organizational integrity.

Most organizations start in the right place. However, for many, checks and balances turn into wildly redundant processes and rules. Every time a new issue is raised, the immediate response is "we should form a committee for that." And before you know it, there are committees deliberating on every trivial issue. Eventually the clarity of direction that the committees were intended to create morphs into a hodgepodge of vague guidelines, white papers, and webinars that leave the individual confused and having to exercise their own discretion and judgment. I have seen thick documents created to describe in detail how to perform tasks like performance reviews, team coaching, and people management. I will go out on a limb and speculate that far fewer people have read those documents than the hundred or so who might read this book. (Pro tip: before adding a new committee, ask if an existing one can tackle the question, or strive for a net-zero increase and find a committee to eliminate.)

The committee rapid-reproduction phenomenon is a source of waste, but it can be contained to management levels. However, the broader organizational impact is that it breeds (and almost encourages) a culture of low accountability at all levels. "Pyramids" are created in the name of professional development. A not-so-junior employee is made responsible for a brand-new employee. A manager delegates their tasks to multiple others. Eventually everyone ends up checking someone else's work. I constantly challenge teams to de-layer. It is more efficient to have fewer people focus on the job at hand than many people owning small fractions of it. Rather than have three people check the work of an associate, it would be better to teach the person to get things done right the first time.

Unfortunately, I see overlayering as all too common in most professional organizations. And we are not talking about the government here; the behavior I describe exists in profit-making companies that you would think would have the most incentive to be as lean as possible. The employees are not at fault. They just clone the culture they see coming from the top. Companies and teams must strive to be as lean as possible without being reckless. Individual accountability is key for the success of any project, program, or initiative. If everyone starts looking to someone else to do their job, then the entire system collapses rapidly. When individual team members constantly challenge themselves to make things leaner and faster, they get to go on to solve more exciting problems.

Thursday, November 12, 2020

To: Compellium Team
From: Samrat Shenbaga
Subject: DEMOCRACIES AND
THE 2021 COMPELLIUM PLAN

Compellium Team:

It was great to "see" many of you at the Compellium town hall and I hope everyone enjoyed it. Happy Diwali to those who celebrate it. As I reflect on the dialog during the town hall, my chest continues to expand with the Pride and Joy of being part of your team. The hunger to out-perform and curiosity to keep getting better is unmatched.

When we were going through the election season in the US and the Compellium planning exercise at the same time, I was reminded of a "Samratism" that I have used as inspiration. Given all the emotion around the election, I didn't want to inject it at an inopportune time. But now that the US election is over (I think), I share it here for your consideration: ***Democracy is deliberately & very smartly designed for steady and incremental change.***

Growing up in India I was always amazed how the government

in my native state of Tamil Nadu would whipsaw every 5 years. The people would overwhelmingly vote the party of the movie star in for a term. And the next time around they would throw him out in favor of the movie star's scriptwriter. And this cycle just went back and forth and continues to present day. I am unsure of the present situation, but during the '90s, in Italy and Japan it felt like the governments changed every weekend. However, the parliamentary system is easy to understand. When I moved to the US, I was utterly confused. I have a mental narrative of the Founding Fathers as they wrote the Constitution.

Franklin: Let's keep this simple, guys, and just do what the Brits do. How about a House that takes care of everything? Let's wrap this up—I am told I have to inaugurate a bridge they want to name after me in Philly.

Jefferson: Well, just for kicks, we should add a Senate. Imagine how happy people would be if we can guarantee employment for at least 2 people in each State.

Washington: That's all good. But I need a job. Let's put something on top of all this—someone who can just keep sending things back.

Madison: May I suggest a Supreme Court, which at any point can throw out the work done by any of the above?

Adams: This is looking great. Let's crack open a 12-pack of my home-brewed Summer Ale and figure out the business rules. Item 1: Who picks the Supreme Court? Item 2: Let each State make up their own rules...

And on and on they go till *Hancock* throws up his hands in exasperation and says, "Enough already! Can we all just sign this darn thing?"

When I was younger, I would get frustrated about why governments could not make quick and obvious moves. But as I have aged and (hopefully) matured, I realize that the inventors of democracy had extraordinary foresight. In my humble opinion, they realized that sudden lurches one way or the other can be dangerous. The system of checks and balances ensures that the people can pull the system back when it is overreaching. The two steps forward, 1.5 steps back approach of democracy magically creates steady, meaningful progress. You'll have to trust me on this one because I have had more than twice the amount of time to observe this phenomenon than most of you.

Now I don't want to claim to be a Founding Father. However, our Compellium business plan/strategy follows the principles of democracy. It is built based on the desires and aspirations of the people on the team. There is ambition in it where we want to try newer areas and ideas, but we also recognize that not all will work out—and that's okay. Our aspiration is for good, steady growth (10%-15%) and to avoid any wild lurches. We've also built many checks and balances within the team to ensure that Compellium is getting a consistent experience from our firm. One major difference from any government is that we want to keep processes light and politics non-existent. 😊 The goal, however, is the same—create opportunity for all, have all voices heard and respected, and ensure that we make steady progress as a team. Hope you are all as excited about the future as I am.

For many, enjoy and relax over an extended weekend. Stay safe and healthy, and as always, let me know if I can be of help. Thanks.

Samrat

■ ■ ■

THE DISCUSSION of the US Constitution always brings to mind for me the argument I hear every four years about how, given the right circumstances, the losing candidate could have won the election if it were decided by the popular vote instead of the electoral college.

I enjoy the game of tennis. According to the rules of tennis, the player who wins the higher number of sets wins the match. How come no one has complained that in five percent of tennis matches the losing player has been robbed because they actually won more points? Case in point is the match between John Isner and Nicolas

Mahut, which is the longest match ever played in the history of professional tennis, clocking in at eleven hours and five minutes—and an astonishing 183 games. John Isner won the match when he captured the final set 70–68. But that is not the most amazing statistic. What most people don't know is that Mahut won a total of 502 points in that match as opposed to Isner's 478. Yet I never heard a legion of tennis experts cry foul about the injustice Mahut had suffered—he definitely did not. The simple fact is that Isner knew what the rules were when he started, and he tailored his strategy to maximize his chances of victory. If Isner had been told that the deciding factor was going to be number of points won instead of sets, he would not have let the second set slip away easily at 6–3; he would have fought for every point. At minimum Isner would have tried not to let 103 of Mahut's relatively average serves get by him for aces.

The same is true for elections. If US presidential elections were decided by the popular vote, then imagine the campaign dollars that would pour into California and New York. Currently the candidates only visit those states for fundraisers with extremely wealthy donors. And good luck to Iowa and New Hampshire ever being on the travel itinerary of a presidential candidate. Politics of course is not a game the way tennis is—there are real-life implications. But candidates know the rules going in. They need to maximize their chances of success with that set of rules; if they don't like them, they need to work to change them for the next match.

In consulting, rules are important too. At the outset of an engagement, we—the client and the consultant together—decide the rules of the game; that is, we write a contract: the deliverables that will be produced, the duties the consultant will perform, the duties the client will perform, the price of the services, and so on.

However, almost without fail, as the project gets going, new facts surface and both parties realize that the actual problem that needs to be solved is different (a little or a lot) from what they originally thought. The consultant can then dig their heels in—they never agreed to this new problem statement—and become obsessed with managing "scope creep." The client, on the other hand, feels the consultant promised to solve anything and everything during the sales pitch. In another case of wasted human capital, the two parties can end up spending many tense moments negotiating what is in and out of scope.

No matter how hard we try to define the "rules" up front, we don't know what we don't know—even if we pretend we do. In my utopia, consultants and clients would sign off on the following agreement: "We both know that things will change. Here is a starting point. We agree that things will be off by plus or minus 25 percent by the time we are done. We will trust each other and not argue about it." If the consultant wants repeat business, they will not push their luck on how much of a premium to charge. And if the client wants the best service, they won't look to pinch pennies. But alas, that would just be too simple!

Wednesday, November 25, 2020

To: Compellium Team
From: Samrat Shenbaga
Subject: DOGS HAVE A LOT
TO BE THANKFUL FOR

Compellium Team:

Hope everyone is getting a break from the frantic pace of work as clients and staffers in the US disperse for Thanksgiving. That translates to fewer emails and a more relaxed pace for all around the globe. While it has been a tough year on different fronts, we have a lot to be thankful for. Perhaps the biggest thing is the compassion and support everyone on the team shows for each other on a daily basis. I am thankful and grateful for being part of a team that is ambitious, thoughtful, conscientious, and most importantly a lot of fun. Each day I am thankful for the Pride and Joy you fill me with.

While we as humans have things to be thankful for, I have always believed household pets have the best of all worlds. Last Wednesday, I woke up to a dog who didn't want to move. And when she did get up, her breathing was incredibly labored. For those who have been around dogs, you know that is a sign of big trouble. So I headed with her to our main vet's office. After many X-rays, I was sent off to the specialty center about a half hour away. 2-3 hours of diagnostics later, the verdict was aspiration pneumonia. Before anyone freaks out, I have attached a picture from this morning that shows Chloe on a good track to recovery. But over the last week I have been wondering if dogs really know all the things they should be thankful for. Below are a few:

- As I pulled into the specialty center, I was greeted by a large complex with multiple buildings. The first one said "Optometry and Dermatology." Then there was oncology followed by radiology succeeded by physical rehab and so on. There was even a sign that advertised acupuncture services. I started wondering how many dogs needed prescriptions for contact lenses. And I couldn't stop myself from thinking that there must be a spa around for pedicures and manicures. If I get sick, I shall go to this place.

- Chloe ended up being hospitalized for two days. Attached is her treatment regimen. Pretty darn impressive.

- As I was checking off on the admission papers, the vet asked, "In the unlikely event your pet crashes, we need your permission to give her CPR." My first thought was "Who is going to give a sick dog CPR? Do they have other dogs trained to administer mouth-to-mouth? Or does a poor intern have to breathe into a dog that has pneumonia?" Again, not sure if my dog realizes how thankful she should be for all the brave souls willing to jump into action.

- From the treatment list, you can imagine the bill was not for the faint of heart. Our company health insurance doesn't cover pets. ☹ As I drove her back home on Friday, I remarked to Chloe, "You should be thankful I didn't follow the concept of ROI we use at work. You do realize that I could have bought 5 of you for the price I just paid?" She ignored the question.

- During the discharge, the nurse told me that they had given Chloe antianxiety meds during her stay and were sending the rest home in case they were needed. The nurse conveniently didn't mention who would be needing the meds. I've been popping them frequently for the past week as I monitor Chloe's breathing, ensure all the medications are administered at the right time, track availability of chicken and rice, and call the hospital back with dumb questions.

Well, it has been a bit of an adventure, but I am thankful that Chloe is on a positive path. My only minor disappointment was when my daughter pointed out after reviewing the bill that the center didn't even bother spelling my name right. (Apparently I am now Semrat Shenbaga.)

With that I am going to kick into low gear for a few days. Hope everyone gets a breather and, where possible, enjoys time with extended family. Thank you for everything you do and for who you are. And let me know if I can be of any help.

Samrat

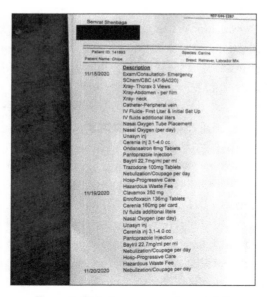

Figure 9. Chloe's very expensive vet visit

Figure 10. Chloe feeling much better

■ ■ ■

THE SUDDEN AND UNEXPECTED events in the veterinary offices brought to mind two beliefs I hold in my professional and personal life. First, it is important to create the best possible conditions in order to ensure the optimal outcomes. However, getting fixated on the outcome itself can lead to hasty decision-making that prioritizes immediate gratification rather than ensures the underlying foundational issues are set up for long-term success. In this case, the best foundation I could lay was to get my dog to the best facility, give the doctors the required guardrails within which I wanted them to operate, and then leave it to the experts to get to the best possible outcome. If I had insisted on a certain length of hospitalization or a specific budget, the wrong choices could have been made.

The second belief I hold is that one should not assume what someone else wants. It is natural to get carried away with a feeling of "this worked so well for me, it must be the right thing for you too." Parents do this to their kids, bosses to their employees, mentors to mentees, coaches to players, and so on. But norms evolve over time, and people's preferences and desires change. While they might appreciate that someone is looking out for them, they can also be equally annoyed if they sense they are being fit into a mold someone else determines is right. In my dog's case, when posed the question of whether I would want her resuscitated, I struggled with "What would *she* want?" Unfortunately, dogs can't speak, but I made a reasonable inference that given her free-spirited personality, she would not want to be kept alive in a miserable state. I spoke for her to the veterinarian, but if vets could speak dog, I would rather have had her communicate her preferences to them directly.

I believe organizations have a responsibility to create the right conditions for everyone to have the opportunity to pursue their path and fulfill their potential. For many years, top-tier consulting firms recruited only from Ivy League schools. They were not trying to discriminate but didn't fully realize that they were cutting out many groups based on their choice of where they sourced talent from. So now many are correcting the conditions by looking for talent across a much broader pool of sources.

Most professional services firms have embraced moves to create parity for all. They take pay parity seriously, have created flexibility for working parents, and invest in unconscious bias training for the entire staff. The positive changes are evident in corporate culture, but there can still be more progress. We will have reached the summit when each employee can say, "I was given a fair shot to get the job I wanted, and the firm provided the right support to make me successful. I've earned this spot fairly, just like everyone else around me has."

In many organizations, these types of initiatives start with the best of intentions. After George Floyd's horrifying death, there were statements from companies that Black lives do matter, that

Black employees do matter, that the company needed to do better at recruiting and nurturing Black employees. Many companies started or enhanced their diversity, equity, and inclusion (DEI) activities. These are all good and true statements and worthwhile efforts. However, organizations must be careful to put programs in place that will be sustained and followed through in the long term. If there is a big push based on one national event and then this push quickly loses steam, employees can feel the company's efforts were disingenuous. Any time a tragic event like the one in Minneapolis occurs (which we hope is rare), the organization should be reminded of the need to look at their entire canvas of equity.

In my opinion, for DEI and similar initiatives to succeed, organizations must hyperfocus on creating the right conditions for everyone, ensuring each person has the opportunity to choose their own path. Recruiting efforts should be spread across a broad spectrum of options. Onboarding should recognize the gaps/disadvantages some groups have and address them. Accommodations should be made for personal constraints; for example, while the corporate world still has a long way to go, there is already marked improvement in allowing employees the flexibility to adapt their schedules for childcare.

Measurement of progress is important. If you are focusing on changing the gender mix and don't measure the gender mix, how do you know if you are making progress? However, as organizations set goals for representation of various groups, they must be cautious in predetermining outcomes.

Perhaps my wife explained the whole issue to me best about a year after we got married. She is a Dartmouth grad, and when I met her, she described herself as a feminist. I presumed that meant that she would want a career of her own, not want to be "dependent" on me, and that I could retire at forty-five while she pursued a CEO-type career. She was a hard-charging high school teacher when we dated and got married. Six months later, she quit her job and stated that she would be a homemaker for life. My dreams of early retirement were doomed. I asked her whether this new stance of hers didn't contradict her being a feminist. I still recall the answer. She confidently stated, "Being a feminist means I get to make my own choices. And I've chosen to be a homemaker." It made me realize that I had a biased view of what she might find to be a meaningful career. She had the right set of conditions so that she could choose her path—multiple opportunities existed for her, but the choice of which one to pick was hers.

Tuesday, December 15, 2020

To: Compellium Team
From: Samrat Shenbaga
Subject: LET ANIMALS BE ANIMALS

Compellium Team:

It is that time of year when many start dispersing for a well-deserved break. It has been quite a year with many zigs and zags. The pride and joy I feel for being part of your team, however, has been on a straight line up. The team feels more connected than ever, despite the physical separation. Sadly, in 2020 some on the team have either experienced the direct effects of the virus or had a family member who was severely impacted. In those cases, I am proud of how the rest of you have supported and consoled your colleagues.

When my daughter was 5 years old, I reluctantly agreed to take her to a "swim with the dolphins" experience on the Big Island in Hawaii. The dolphins were in a modest-sized lagoon right next to the ocean. The instructor was an enthusiastic, young animal lover. She proudly launched into a monologue on how well the dolphins were cared for at the venue, how they lived longer than out in the wild, how they had excellent healthcare, etc. After a few minutes I couldn't resist and asked, "How do you really know these dolphins are happy? They are just swimming around in circles in this small lagoon. Each time they jump, they see the vast, open ocean where their friends are leaping freely." The instructor looked aghast, the remaining attendees murmured their annoyance, and afterwards my daughter (who is bcc'd) gave me a stern talking to (I recall being asked "What is wrong with you?"). Many reprimands have since been issued on other transgressions.

That story leads me to the last Samratism of the year: **The happiest pets are the "worst" behaved.** If you visit Disney World and decide to stop by my house, you will be greeted by two Labrador retrievers who will charge at you full speed, climb on you, lick your face, and leave enough hair on your clothes for a mini blanket. No amount of "sit" or "get down" will dissuade them. I do not apologize for such behavior, as their happiness takes precedence over that of the traumatized guests. Between my two dogs, the older one, Riley, is more independent-minded. When he was a puppy, we were concerned that he was hard of hearing as he didn't pay attention to anything that was said. Then we suspected he had poor vision as he appeared not to notice the signs being given to him. Eventually we realized that he just didn't give a damn. I have a habit of celebrating odd milestones. Today marks Riley's 100-month birthday! During that time, this dog has cost me between 1,000 and 2,000 hours of my life. A simple example is when I let him out in the yard to do his business and want him to come back in. It is a 15-minute ordeal each time. If dogs could control their toes, I fully expect that when I say, "Time to come back in, buddy," he would raise a front paw and point up his middle toe. And it is guaranteed that when I tell him not to go in the pool, he will take it as the cue to enjoy a 30-minute swim. But his wildness does make it fun, and we've had lots of good times together.

Note: Let me quickly address a question that might have popped up: *How does Samrat justify constraining dogs to a house/yard when he complains about domesticated dolphins?* I don't know the history of dogs, but I suspect their natural state is to be with humans. I've seen my dogs chase squirrels, bunnies, birds, but never have they caught a single thing. Not a good look for a species that is not vegetarian. There is a reason they are tagged as "retrievers" and not "hunters."

Having spent time with this team, my wish for each of you is that you continue to be your own selves. Don't feel compelled to fit into a standard track that others say is the best path. There are many definitions of "good," and you have to pick your own. From a business perspective, I measure our client success by intangibles such as: are people getting growth opportunities, does the team feel okay taking risk, are we letting ideas thrive? Each of you is special in many ways; keep cultivating that part of you. The coming year will bring many opportunities, professional and personal, to let your adventurous side fly.

With that, I wish you and yours a Happy Holiday season and a Happy New Year. Use the appropriate caution when celebrating as there is still a pandemic around us. Hope the holidays give you time to recharge and return in 2021 ready to infuse a lot of Riley wildness. As always, let me know if I can be of any help.

Samrat

Figure 11. Poor dolphin

Figure 12. Happy dog

Figure 13. If I could control my toes...

■ ■ ■

CONSULTING FIRMS tend to have "cult" cultures. They recruit a certain type of personality, reinforce specific values by having leaders embody them, and consistently demonstrate their firm's desired image in interactions with clients. My firm has a down-to-earth, no-flash, focus-on-the-client personality. When I was new to the firm, I was puzzled by a senior partner who would keep a Dodge Eagle in the office parking lot. He would drive into the office in his beautiful Maserati, but any time we had to head to a client location, we would all pile into his Dodge Eagle. Over time, I learned that regardless of how much money this partner was making, he didn't want to appear ostentatious; we needed to stay focused on the work being done and not create potential distractions for the client. I've always remembered that lesson.

Maintaining a culture is important to an organization. However, getting stuck in it can be counterproductive. Popular culture evolves over time and is a living, breathing thing. As an example, at the beginning of Obama's presidency he was a firm naysayer on gay marriage (and stated so explicitly in the debates leading up to his election). But by the end of his eight years, Obama had moved to where the country stood on the issue. We are living in an age of heightened sensitivity to sexism, homophobia, and racism. What feels perfectly fine today will not be appropriate in a few years.

Firm leaders often confuse culture with values. Culture needs to morph and adapt to the times, especially as companies get bigger, open new lines of business, and attract a more diverse set of employees. For many years at my firm, we grew our leaders from inside the firm. I started as an associate and worked my way up to partner; that was the norm. We were unsure how we would integrate someone if they joined directly at the partner level, and as a result were quite conservative in senior-level hiring. But as the firm grew, the downsides of this approach started becoming apparent: there was not as much diversity of thought or experience when everyone followed the same path of progression. It was also challenging for clients to perceive us as credible when we presented them with new ideas, because they had seen us in only one light for the entirety of our careers. So we instituted changes for integrating experienced hires, created support structures around them, and made existing partners responsible for the success of those we hired in.

Values, on the other hand, are nonnegotiable. Typically, a company's values statement delineates the quality of product offered, the feeling a client/customer should get, and how the firm will operate, including the treatment employees can expect. There is no single "correct" set of values—as consultants like to say, "It depends." For one firm, ensuring customer satisfaction could be the primary value. For another, while they may want happy customers, they value employee work-life balance more highly. Regardless of what the values are, they must be specific and clear to everyone in the firm; any violations must be met with immediate consequences.

If leadership can declare its values, walk the talk, and hire people who will live and breathe those values in their professional lives, then management has little to worry about. All they need to do is get out of the way and watch their firm succeed and thrive.

Monday, January 11, 2021

To: Compellium Team
From: Samrat Shenbaga
Subject: TIME TO REV UP OUR ENGINES

Compellium Team:

Hope you had a great break and are re-energized for the New Year. My biggest source of pride and joy during the break was that everyone on the team committed to chilling out. Vaccination news across the globe has started heating up, which provides a glimmer of hope, and I expect it will accelerate us back towards normalcy in the coming months. There will still be ups and downs, but hopefully the good news slowly starts outweighing the negative vibes.

I once estimated that I had spent over 100k miles driving on the freeways of Southern California between LA (the original office I started in), Orange County (where the clients are), and San Diego (where I lived and opened the office). And during my career I have racked up thousands of miles between various offices and client locations. During these distances traveled I have become somewhat of a ***car & driver profiler.***

For example, I could be whizzing along in the fast lane at 75 MPH on a lightly busy I-405 and come up behind a 2007 light gold Toyota Camry that is coasting at 63 MPH (exactly 2 MPH below the speed limit). No amount of nudging up to the Camry or flashing the headlights is going to get it to move over. Instead, the best course of action is to shift to the middle lane and pass. If I look over, I have a 50%+ chance of seeing a 63-year-old lady who is sitting upright in the driver's seat, which is pulled up as close to the steering wheel as physically possible, and she is looking straight ahead without any need for rearview mirrors. On the flip side, there are times when I will be cranking away on an empty freeway with no one behind me—and a 2015 dark gray Honda Odyssey Sport will suddenly appear in my rearview mirror with less than 6 inches separating it from my rear bumper. In this case, it is wisest to move over and let the stressed out, road-raging 37-year-old guy speed by—good chance his Sunday afternoon football game viewings were jarringly upended three years ago with the unexpected arrival of twins. The theory is confirmed when I catch a glimpse of the "Baby on Board" and "Pittsburgh Steelers" stickers on his rear window as he flashes by.

The most soothing feeling on the freeway is when I catch a glimpse of a 2003 blue Dodge Neon in my rear- or side-view mirror. (For those in India who are unfamiliar with the venerable Dodge Neon, think of it as an old Maruti 800.) This brings me to the first Samratism of 2021: ***The car with the most horsepower isn't the fastest one on the freeway.*** As I watch this car behind me, I am mesmerized by the ease with which it weaves across lanes, turns on its blinkers (not to ask for permission but just to let the other driver know what is happening), and, one by one, gets ahead of Ford F-150s, BMW 3 Series, Lincoln Continentals, etc. It doesn't matter which lane I am in or what speed I am going—I do not need to do a thing. In the next 3 minutes I am guaranteed to have this car in front of me. When it glides by and I look over, I will see a 19-year-old kid with windows rolled down, one hand on the steering wheel and the other hanging out the window, and possibly their left foot folded up. This kid is free, has no fear, and is the master of the road. He or she is slicing through the freeway like a hot knife through butter and optimizing their drive in real time. If everyone were like them, there would be no traffic jams.

Our business is a little bit like the cars on the freeway. We as a team and as a company are a pretty well-oiled machine—and we have become a high-horsepower, luxury brand. Clients love us for our responsiveness and reliability. This was a big part of our success in 2020 when, during a time of heavy uncertainty, clients turned to partners like us who they could bank on. However, the risk for a luxury automotive like us is that we can get overtaken by a free-wheeling group of smart newbies who have no fear and are willing to take more risks. The scary part is that they can creep up in our rearview mirror and get ahead of us before we even realize it. So it becomes paramount for us to keep our edge and not get too comfortable with our success. In all areas of our business, in addition to delivering high quality work, we will have to recommit to stripping down our machinery so that it doesn't lose its nimbleness. And we want to add just enough recklessness so that we are surprising clients without creating a major crash.

If you haven't spent your December bonus yet, maybe this note has inspired you to look for a vintage Dodge Neon or Maruti 800! I look forward to an exciting ride in 2021 for all of us. Continue to stay vigilant during the pandemic. I am sure, just like me, most of you have pandemic fatigue in addition to Zoom fatigue. But we are at the beginning of the end—we have been disciplined so far, and surely we can hold on a bit longer. Take care and, as always, let me know if I can be of any help.

Samrat

■ ■ ■

INCUMBENCY IS A common problem in life. Inevitably, with the passage of time people get bored with the incumbent. To warrant their survival the incumbent must be greatly loved by the masses or somehow keep things exciting. Sometimes the new source of excitement is met with grumbling, yet after a few short moments (or news cycles), the grumbling turns into applause for the incumbent's courage.

Car models are a good example. Consumers fall in love with a particular model, are comfortable with its features, appreciate the pleasing aesthetics, and swear they will keep repurchasing the same model in the future. However, every six or seven years the manufacturer springs a redesign on the consumer. I have rarely seen a new model met with resounding applause. Existing customers complain about how the position of the cupholders has changed, aficionados make nostalgic observations about the classic appeal being gone, and technical experts critique the new navigation system. But without fail, as the newer models start appearing on the road, the previous models start looking ancient—even if purchased just the previous year. Neighbors start asking current owners, "Are you going to get the new one?" And soon CarMax is flooded with the now-suddenly-stale prior model. Manufacturers realize that there is a diminishing-returns curve to the excitement a product can generate and that at some point the sentiment for the product could even go into reverse. Even though it sometimes seems that change has been done only for change's sake, it is important for survival.

The more toxic by-product of incumbency is complacency. It is a phenomenon commonly seen with political parties across the globe. The populace gives an overwhelming verdict in favor of a party. For the first year or two, the party pushes forth ambitiously with its newfound fortune. But typically, an inflection point comes around the eighteen-month mark: the new leaders get comfortable. They assume that the electorate will be satisfied with "good enough." More often than not, they also attempt pet projects that have nothing to do with their original mandate. And then, without fail, in a couple of years the fed-up electorate swings the pendulum to the other side.

Much of what afflicts car manufacturers and politicians holds true for the business world as well. A significant amount of energy is invested in winning new business. The firm's experts are put on display, disruptive ideas are presented, and a sense of purpose is established for the client-consultant relationship. Things usually get off to a blistering start—the customer is excited about the new relationship, and the consulting partner wants to get off on the right foot. If there are conflicts, even small ones, the most senior people from the consulting firm jump in to resolve them. Over time, the relationship settles. The consultant gets a better understanding of the client's organizational dynamics and forms opinions of what will fly versus what will be squashed on introduction. A focus on project profitability begins to weigh on the consultant. Slowly they move from trying to do "everything to please" to "let's be good enough."

This behavior is even more true of the more established consultants. They've worked in their respective industries long enough to know the ins and outs and to realize that most clients' needs are 80 percent the same. They offer core services with limited customization, much like a Cadillac offers the Escalade: the customer can choose color, seat material, sound system options, and so on, but the engine, transmission, and body are set. If a client is "too much trouble"—that is, wants too much customization—these firms can make the decision to "fire" the customer and move on.

The problem for these established firms is the younger version of them that can creep up without notice. No matter how satisfied clients are, they always suffer from wanderlust. They also want to keep consultants on their toes so that they don't take the client's business for granted. The young gunslinger firms have a lot to gain and not much to lose. Often, they are not worried about short-term profitability and are willing to bend to a client's every wish. Seasoned consultants often tell their clients they should be nimble and agile but forget the lesson themselves.

Good business leaders are always thinking several steps ahead. They challenge their teams with questions like "If the client asked us today why we deserve this business, how would we demonstrate our value to them?" or "Instead of getting bigger, should we be splitting ourselves into smaller pieces to maintain our edge?" Injecting a sense of healthy paranoia is helpful in sustaining and growing the business, but the bigger impact I see is that team members are energized. If bright, young, aspiring folks are told "Just don't screw it up—maintain the base quality we are supposed to hit," they quickly become uninspired and uninterested. They become comfortable in a system and fall into the "let me collect my paycheck" trap. If challenged with the "What should we change?" mantra, it piques their natural curiosity and increases their ownership of a task or project. Not every idea a freshly minted college graduate brings to the table will fly. But more often than not, I am surprised how they point out things that I had stopped seeing because I was blinded by my twenty-five years of industry experience.

Thursday, February 4, 2021

To: Compellium Team
From: Samrat Shenbaga
Subject: SAMRATISMS ARE GOING EMERITUS

Compellium Team:

I am sensing a shift in mood. More and more of my conversations with clients, friends, colleagues, and family now start with "This person I know just got the vaccine" (as opposed to "So and so person I know got the virus"). I find myself obsessively checking the daily Florida vaccination report (attached) instead of refreshing the Worldometer page every hour. The other day when I was at the golf course, an older member walked right up to me to introduce himself with a fist bump. The last 12 months of training made me recoil in horror as I saw him approaching, but clearly he had been vaccinated and felt the world was back to normal. I enjoyed the little experience and then immediately doused my hand with Purell once he turned around. Not to say that we are out of the woods—not by a long stretch. There are bound to be bumps in the road in the coming weeks and months. However, we can take comfort in little nuggets like the fact that more people in the US and UK have now entered the vaccination funnel than were diagnosed— and that gap gets bigger each day as the vaccination rates increase and infection rates decrease. In India, there is cautious optimism that the worst is behind us as people slowly venture out. So let's keep our optimistic lenses on and just maybe start planning our late summer vacations. ☺

Around this time of year a few beloved firm principals enter the emeritus program. It is a recognition of their amazing accomplishments and their desire to move to the next phase of their lives. In the same spirit, I figure it is time to send "Samratisms" to emeritus status. For one, I don't have many left. Secondly, all things run their course. And lastly, it poses an intriguing challenge for me to think of something new to include in these communications. While the Samratisms will go emeritus, the pride and joy I feel for everything you have done and continue to do will never retire—it only continues to grow.

Here is the last Samratism: ***A public works construction project has no end.*** Case in point is Carmel Valley Road at the intersection of SR-56 in San Diego, CA. In the 10+ years that I used this intersection, there was always some activity that would slow down traffic due to diversions, or flatten the tire of every 1000th vehicle due to a construction nail. For the first 3 years, they were building it out as new neighborhoods started appearing in the area. Just when they were done, they realized there were more neighborhoods than originally thought—and hence, an extra lane had to be added. That went on for 2 years. Hardly had the new tar dried than there was an awakening that the sewer system needed more capacity. Off they went digging up everything, diverting traffic for 18 months as they brought in new pipes. And just when the water pressure in the showers reached an acceptable level for the residents, an idea was floated to reduce congestion at the onramp by adding a carpool lane. Off we went again. And this is not just a San Diego, CA, phenomenon. Same is true for the I95, I4, I70, I5, I405—put any number against an I. Engineers embark on an expansion or modernization project based on increased traffic volume → project runs for 10 years → at the end of 10 years, planners realize now the traffic is even higher → rinse and repeat. Nor is this a uniquely American phenomenon. My father tells me every week about how the corporation in Coimbatore has decided to drill holes for the wildest of reasons into a road they built just 6 months ago. In one mind-blowing experiment, they put an electric pole right in the middle of the street (and yes, 6 months later they came back to move it to the side of the street).

What does all this have to do with us? As you know, there is only one degree of separation between a Samratism and our firm. The part of this Samratism that we should strive for is one of continuous improvement. When something is done, we should resist the urge to sit back and admire it. We should immediately think of how we can make it better. The part we should maniacally avoid is of short-sighted planning. Clients rely on us to help them think two steps ahead. The immediate request they might have is "reassess my sales force size." Anyone can do that for them. What we need to help them with is to plan for what happens once the sales force is smaller or bigger. No client wants to be told at the end of a project that we have a new problem to show them just to start another project. Many times just asking the client all the questions they should be thinking about adds way more value than one would think.

2021 is off to a good start on the business front, and I see many opportunities for us to work with Compellium on. That in turn will give each of us new areas to explore. Of course, we need to continue to be vigilant and safe as the pandemic (hopefully) winds down. The key now is patience and we should be able to get on the other side. Take care and, as always, let me know if I can be of any help.

Samrat

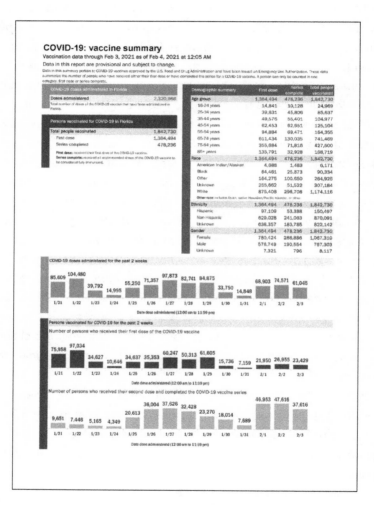

Figure 14. Florida vaccine report (page 1)

COVID-19: vaccine summary

Vaccination data through Feb 3, 2021 as of Feb 4, 2021 at 12:05 AM

Data in this report are provisional and subject to change.

This table is the number of people who received their first dose or completed their COVID-19 vaccine series yesterday and cumulatively by county of residence.

County of residence	Yesterday (Feb 3)			Cumulative		
	First dose	Series complete	Total people vaccinated	First dose	Series complete	Total people vaccinated
Alachua	394	549	943	22,284	13,091	35,375
Baker	58	28	86	1,508	324	1,832
Bay	199	168	367	13,061	1,139	14,200
Bradford	190	15	205	1,728	280	2,008
Brevard	583	614	1,197	38,006	12,182	50,288
Broward	1,340	2,866	4,206	108,941	41,857	150,798
Calhoun	78	37	115	1,287	251	1,538
Charlotte	337	131	468	13,735	3,305	17,040
Citrus	74	231	305	12,890	2,704	15,594
Clay	400	711	1,111	10,550	4,521	15,071
Collier	92	468	560	36,345	6,485	42,830
Columbia	29	52	81	3,257	1,503	4,760
Dade	2,248	6,550	8,883	111,736	74,019	185,755
Desoto	24	41	65	2,253	386	2,639
Dixie	4	7	11	828	128	956
Duval	354	3,095	3,449	59,961	24,954	84,915
Escambia	229	372	601	22,501	5,961	28,462
Flagler	180	58	238	9,451	2,349	11,800
Franklin	7	61	68	1,152	214	1,366
Gadsden	29	170	199	4,024	1,103	5,127
Gilchrist	33	28	61	1,075	397	1,472
Glades	2	219	221	337	270	607
Gulf	5	75	80	1,403	238	1,639
Hamilton	3	4	7	1,110	45	1,155
Hardee	18	114	132	1,126	238	1,364
Hendry	6	65	71	1,448	607	2,055
Hernando	465	518	983	12,632	2,962	15,594
Highlands	19	117	136	5,583	1,024	6,607
Hillsborough	1,003	3,809	4,812	53,310	29,939	83,249
Holmes	2	53	55	947	638	1,585
Indian River	23	138	161	17,939	2,701	20,640
Jackson	47	354	401	3,439	1,620	5,059
Jefferson	59	166	225	1,512	403	1,915
Lafayette	1	3	4	677	51	728
Lake	96	114	210	27,247	12,471	39,718
Lee	407	399	806	52,437	14,710	67,147
Leon	508	674	1,182	20,947	9,595	30,542
Levy	34	30	64	2,365	519	2,884
Liberty	12	17	29	676	63	739
Madison	63	120	183	1,830	385	2,215
Manatee	1,204	456	1,660	19,887	9,352	29,239
Marion	977	377	1,354	27,338	6,527	33,865
Martin	57	298	356	16,695	4,051	20,746
Monroe	20	455	475	5,073	2,103	7,176
Nassau	78	203	281	8,407	1,571	9,978
Okaloosa	304	254	558	13,809	2,915	16,724
Okeechobee	13	195	208	2,133	606	2,739
Orange	809	946	1,755	63,921	28,153	92,074
Osceola	488	107	595	15,413	4,992	20,405
Out-Of-State	248	530	778	50,453	7,289	57,742
Palm Beach	2,436	3,946	6,382	139,668	34,905	174,573
Pasco	828	683	1,511	26,745	9,691	36,436
Pinellas	2,638	1,566	4,204	61,681	22,343	84,024
Polk	776	457	1,233	31,598	6,847	38,445
Putnam	52	37	89	3,969	651	4,620
Santa Rosa	719	299	1,018	13,898	4,209	18,107
Sarasota	621	297	918	34,928	11,123	46,051
Seminole	454	704	1,158	26,424	12,680	39,104
St. Johns	76	639	715	27,582	7,895	35,257
St. Lucie	151	257	408	20,493	6,265	26,758
Sumter	174	299	473	18,537	2,371	20,908
Suwannee	197	19	216	3,335	526	3,859
Taylor	95	368	464	1,417	464	1,881
Union	49	6	55	887	128	1,015
Unknown	39	24	63	1,187	391	1,578
Volusia	138	569	707	35,151	13,179	48,330
Wakulla	8	44	52	2,595	578	3,173
Walton	213	129	342	6,417	573	6,990
Washington	8	29	37	1,447	448	1,895
Total	23,429	37,616	61,045	1,364,494	478,236	1,842,730

Figure 14. Florida vaccine report (page 2)

Figure 15. Poles in the middle of the road (yes, really)

■ ■ ■

CONSULTING IS THE ULTIMATE "what have you done for me lately?" business. Clients pay a premium to hire a consultant to deliver high-quality results. Often a consultant leads a client through a major transformation that completely changes the complexion of the company. Once they are past the initial shock and inertia, clients love it. At that moment consultants are at a fork in the road. They can either sit back and bask in the glory of what they have accomplished—or they can figure out the next area of the client's business they can improve. Otherwise, within six months what was "new and exciting" will become "just what everyone else does" and the client will berate the consultant for not having any new ideas.

Some people use the analogy of sandcastles: you build one on the beach, it gets washed away overnight, and then you build a better and bigger one the next day. I quite hate that analogy as it implies that the consultant is deliberately building a product that won't last. Why not move the castle a hundred feet back in the first place? I like the analogy of a sports coach better. The first thing a tennis coach teaches you is to get the ball over the net and get comfortable with your swing as you move the racquet "low to high." Then comes moving your feet, followed by baseline forehands, followed by backhands, and so on and so forth. Each time a student gets comfortable with one aspect of the game, it is time to add another component.

Another dilemma that consultants are faced with is clients constantly asking for ideas that will give them a competitive advantage. During my entire professional life, I have constantly received that request. However, in almost every instance when I have gone to a client with an idea, the first reaction I've gotten is "This sounds great. Who else has done it and how did it work out?" Those are the most frustrating words for a consultant to hear. By definition, companies cannot get a competitive advantage if they always want their competitors to go first!

While it is easy to get discouraged, I have learned that, in the business world, in order to get a 2 percent change, one must propose a 10 percent transformation; only then will people agree to the 2 percent. If one starts out with a proposal for a 2 percent change, then nothing will happen. One of the founders of my firm once wrote me a simple note after a significant accomplishment in my career. It stated, "Great job with the office opening. Swing for the fences." I have always kept those few words in mind. He did not say, "Hit home runs." What I believe he meant was: "Only if you swing for the fences do you have a chance to get singles and doubles, plus the occasional home run. And if you strike out a few times, that's okay—at least you know you tried." I never really asked him if I'd interpreted his words correctly, but I can confirm that my version has served me well.

Leaders have to help their teams understand the trade-offs that inevitably have to be made in the business world. The grass can always look greener on the other side when a young team member is feeling the frustration of a lost weekend due to a project deadline and sees friends from another firm enjoying the same weekend at the beach. However, they might not realize that their extra effort is making a meaningful difference in their career trajectory, or that next month the tables will be reversed when they are at the beach instead.

A misconception in the business world is that leaders must choose between being kind and compassionate to people and driving strong business results. There is an image that someone who achieves terrific business results must be ruthless while someone who is nice doesn't care about the numbers. These are not discrete choices. On the contrary, I view one as a necessary condition to the other. In order to be a strong business leader, one must display a reasonable level of appreciation and empathy towards team members. For one, it is a requirement of being a business professional that one be respectful and kind to their colleagues. For a business leader, there is a bigger incentive. Any successful leader has achieved their big wins on the shoulders of great team members. These team members are in short supply, and every leader is competing to get them. It is in the selfish interest of the leader to make their team members feel good, proud, and successful so that they want to keep working with that leader. If the team flies the coop, the leader's value plummets and achieving any type of business success becomes exponentially harder.

At the same time, pampering teams with endless praise and treats is not helpful. When my daughter was in kindergarten, she returned home with a participation medal after "Olympic day." As all parenting books instruct, I mustered up all my energy to enthusiastically congratulate her. She shrugged her shoulders as she tossed the medal aside and said, "Well, they just give that out to everyone." It could just be a genetic trait of Shenbagas, but I believe most humans are like my daughter. There is a built-in competitive engine in humans and a desire to be showcased only when we've done something that truly stands out. It is the same with teams. A leader must make the distinction between that which is part of the job and that which is above and beyond. Often, I will smile to myself when I am copied on emails to a team by a manager saying, "You are so awesome. This month you got all the reports right." Last I checked that's what the contract with the client calls for. If we make a mistake, then there is a financial penalty. A bigger problem is that the manager has lowered the bar to where the team thinks it might be okay to let an error or two slip through. It is the same reason I don't like it when there's an airline accident and the airplane manufacturer claims their planes have flown thousands of flights without an incident. That is no comfort to the families of the passengers who died. When I board a commercial aircraft, barring an act of god, I expect the manufacturer and airline to ensure 100 percent safety.

Leaders must keep a finger on the emotional pulse of their team. It is best to offer appropriate appreciation and recognition proactively. If done as an afterthought, it feels contrived. At the same time, each leader must set a bar high enough that teams recognize that a reward is truly special. On the flip side, if they sense any form of entitlement, leaders must be ready to communicate the harsh reality of the business world to their team. In these cases, if leaders hesitate to redirect their teams, they will be left with much more drastic and unpleasant choices down the road.

Some leaders describe their approach to managing their team's performance as "carrot and stick"—reward and punishment. I don't like that description, as we are not taming rabbits and donkeys in the business world. These are seasoned professionals with intrinsic aspirations. The job of the leader is to serve as the captain of the ship who has the ultimate responsibility for the direction of the boat—and if the captain knows there's an iceberg, they'd better take action rather than wait for their second-in-command to give them a recommendation.

Friday, February 26, 2021

To: Compellium Team
From: Samrat Shenbaga
Subject: A MEMORABLE WEEK

Compellium Team:

Hope you are well. Now that Samratisms are retired, I am going to shift to **_Random sharing and ramblings by the CSL._** I'll share what I deem to be interesting events in my life or things that are nagging me. Let's think of it as a running personal diary. This last week has been a kind of fun one for me. I eagerly await February 20 every year as it is my daughter's birthday. The first reason for being excited is obvious—it is her birthday. The second, more selfish reason is that I have a tradition by which I go to my favorite restaurant on February 20 and order myself a Remy Martin Louis XIII. In the world of Cognac, the Louis XIII stands alone at the very top. People have asked me whether it wouldn't be cheaper for me to invest in a bottle than pay the ridiculously high price for a pour once a year. Financially that would be a smart move. However, I suspect that if I did purchase a bottle, then I would invent a celebration every couple of weeks ("I just finished time entry—time for a Remy!") and the bottle would be gone in no time. 😕

The toast serves two purposes. One, it is a celebration of a father seeing his only daughter grow up. The second motivator is a sense of relief—I have gone one more year without screwing up my parental duties, and I have one less year of having that responsibility! Depending on the year, one factor outweighs the other. In pursuit of my Louis XIII, I finally ventured to my favorite restaurant in Orlando, called Christini's, after a gap of 11 months. I admit it was a bold move and not one I would recommend, but I was resolved to continue my tradition (virus be damned). Once I went through the main door of the restaurant, I seemed to enter a parallel universe. There was no pandemic there— the place was packed, clientele were having a good time, servers had masks on, but many were using them as chin guards. After the initial recoil, I dove into the false sense of normalcy. Now I am checking my temperature every 3 hours waiting for the virus to makes its appearance—6 days on, so far, so good.

February 22 was far more exciting. In the state of Florida, kids get their driver's learning permit when they turn 15. My daughter made sure she got hers with the first appointment available on Monday. Due to various Zoom calls, I wasn't able to join her first couple of drives around the neighborhood with my wife. Then finally yesterday we went out together in my car. Secretly I have been hoping to upgrade my car, so I figure if she loves the current one, then I can palm it off on her. Barring some very hard braking at stop signs and unnecessary slowing down whenever a squirrel was spotted a hundred yards away, it was a pretty good drive. I am looking forward to when she can get out on the major roads. She can drive me to Christini's, read a book in the parking lot while I enjoy my meal, and drive me back!

And then finally I have been looking for ways to get away from the doom and gloom of "mainstream" media. So I have now become a regular reader of *The Sun*. I am not really sure if what they report is true, but it sure is fun. For three days I was fascinated by the story of the mum who took off with her daughter's boyfriend. There are a lot of inspiring stories about Captain Tom.[38] And today there are a number of pieces showcasing media interviews with Harry, where he is complaining about the media not respecting his privacy (go figure). It does make the UK look like a happening place. Even if 20% of what *The Sun* reports is factual, then I should be looking for a transfer to the London office.

That's the end of my random sharing. Not every week is so exciting, so don't worry about your inbox being flooded with spam from me. Before I close, I must express the constant Pride and Joy I feel for being part of this team. We are engaged in many high-impact programs for our client. We've also hit a couple of road bumps. But even there the team has re-dedicated itself to solving problems collaboratively. Have a good weekend.

Samrat

Figure 16. Remy Martin. Mmmmm.

---

[38] Captain Sir Thomas Moore, a.k.a. Captain Tom, was a British Army officer who served in India and the Burma campaign during the Second World War. During the pandemic, at the age of ninety-nine, he began to walk 100 lengths of his garden to raise money for charity. His goal was to reach £1,000 by his 100th birthday; he raised over £30 million.

■ ■ ■

IN LIFE AND WORK, pausing to enjoy the big moments is important. The corporate hamster wheel is exhausting. Busy leaders work hard throughout the year to hit the various business goals in front of them. They go through highs when an important milestone is reached or a minor hurdle overcome, and then they hit crushing lows if a project fails or a new piece of business does not materialize. Their finance teams closely track performance with weekly and monthly sales and profit reports, which can become all-consuming and addictive.

Just when the leader is ready to celebrate a successful year, it is time to plan for the next year when the clock resets. One starts fretting in September whether the business will be off to a strong start in January, the various scenarios that must be planned for, which people on the team need to be reassigned to new responsibilities, and on and on. Before they know it, the leader misses the opportunity to savor their amazing accomplishments and celebrate with their teams.

When I reflect on my own "mind allocation," I must spend 25 percent of the time fretting over business performance, 25 percent analyzing business performance, and 50 percent driving business performance. There is a near-zero allocation to celebrating business performance. In an ideal world, we should spend 10 percent of our time measuring performance, 75 percent driving performance, and 15 percent celebrating it.

Additionally, leaders should plan celebrations in anticipation of the event rather than after it occurs. Often someone will say, "We hit $100 million—what should we do to celebrate?" Instead, it would be much more satisfying if at the beginning of the year a leader announced, "If we hit $100 million, we are all going to do X." Having something to look forward to is a great motivator for the team, and the act of planning for the potential celebration is in itself a team bonding experience. And once the goal is reached, everyone has a chance to exhale, reflect, and have a blast.

A common concern: "What if we don't hit the target? Won't it be deflating that people don't get the reward they were looking for?" I find that to be a weak excuse. Not planning for success could signal to the team that the leader is not confident in the team's abilities or in the goal that has been set. However, the concern has some merit, so I make the following suggestions:

Don't miss the target and celebrate anyway. Saying "Well, we got to $95 million, which is not bad, and we did all this planning, so let's go ahead and throw the party anyway" sets a poor precedent for the next goal. This year you missed by 5 percent; what if next year the target is missed by 6 percent? Is that okay to celebrate too? Instead of serving as a motivator, the entire celebration becomes "business as usual" and loses its special touch.

Consider ranges instead of point estimates. It is perfectly okay to say "If we land between $98 million and $101 million, that will be awesome as it sets us up well for the future." After all, circumstances change and targets need some flex.

In addition to a monetary target, consider other factors that indicate success. It is difficult to get away from revenues or profits as the measure of success in for-profit businesses. However, leaders must emphasize to their teams that they value movement on different levers of the business even if they are not tied to immediate revenue numbers. For example, a measure of success could be breaking into a new line of business that has eluded the team for the past couple of years, or building relationships with new strategic customers, or diversifying the business portfolio such that there is more balance. To generate excitement for the team, it is important to make the objectives sound inspirational. However, there should be clear outcomes tied to these objectives so that teams know when they have accomplished their goal. For instance, "We strive to be trusted partners to our clients" is a legitimate goal. The only small problem is that each person can interpret "trusted" and "partner" differently. An equally inspirational and tangible goal would be "We want clients to consider us their partner of choice for the major transformation they have embarked on."

Finally, *I suggest leaders celebrate themselves from time to time* and pat their own backs. Team members are often reluctant to shower their leader with praise, as they worry it will be viewed as "kissing up," so it is up to leaders to raise a toast to themselves—and that can be done in the privacy of their own living rooms. Trust me, I have had a few toasts with the only witnesses being my two exhausted dogs!

Tuesday, March 16, 2021

To: Compellium Team
From: Samrat Shenbaga
Subject: CELEBRATING RESILIENCE

Compellium Team:

I am back with more ***Random sharing and ramblings by the CSL.***
Yesterday was "Resilience Day" here at the firm and to celebrate I made
a trip to Christini's. As I consumed their delicious eggplant parmesan,
I couldn't help but fill up with Pride and Joy for being part of this team.
Each of you has worked through challenging situations over the past
year to deliver outstanding value for clients. And you have done so
while fostering a culture of collaboration and respect. Well done! As I
got to dessert, my mind wandered off to some random topics.

- **:25 and :55 isn't working.** On paper it is a good idea to
  schedule meetings to end before the hour or half hour to
  give people time to stretch. Now it could just be me, but in
  the old days, as the clock was ticking closer to :30 or :00,
  people would say, "We only have a minute or two remain-

ing, so let me wrap up." With the :25 and :55, I find people often saying, "Do you have 5 minutes more?" They know those 5 minutes exist—after all, who schedules a call from :25 to :30 or :55 to :00? If :25 and :55 is going to work, then Zoom has to automatically shut off.

- **"Sorry, I was on mute."** If somebody hasn't already, a lot of money is going to be made when the rights are bought for those 5 words. The phrase will appear on T-shirts, coffee mugs, iPhone covers, you name it. After a full year of Zoom working, the mute button continues to be the single biggest challenge for us to overcome. IT should roll out a plug-in that lights up the entire laptop in red when one has their microphone muted. Surely we won't have muting problems then...

- **Chat is stressing me out.** The PAM team got an earful from me on the topic. It is bad enough that I have to check my text messages, read *The Sun,* and track the stock market, all while attending a Zoom call. But the chats just push me over the edge. Is anyone really paying attention to the meeting if people are busy banging away on chat? I vote to get rid of chat and force people to say it.

- **T20[39] is a head scratcher.** On Sunday morning, I watched the England vs. India T20 and I was stumped. If there was a T20 equivalent in soccer, the rules would be modified to something like this: The game is only 15 minutes long → Every time the ball crosses the midfield line, that counts as a goal, hence resulting in a score of 63-57 → and every 45 seconds there is a commercial break for a cell phone plan, car, or bank service to transfer money to India. Secondly, it was a bit jarring to see thousands of people packed into the

---

[39] T20 is a cricket tournament. The T20 format came into being in the early 2000s to provide audiences a four-hour version of a cricket match compared to the traditional full-day and five-day formats. The matches move from venue to venue.

stadium screaming at the top of their lungs. This thing shifts to Pune soon, and I broke into a sweat imagining a scene where Niladri, Mansi, Pranav, and Anuja are caught on camera jumping up and down holding up a "Compellium Team loves Virushka" banner. And lastly, how much does India pay their specialist, duck-scoring[40] opening batsman? This guy is unbelievable—all you have to do is swing your bat wildly in T20 and a boundary[41] is guaranteed. Yet this guy works real hard to guide the ball perfectly into the wicket keeper's gloves.

Not much to take away from this list of ramblings other than don't stress out, take the appropriate precautions against the virus, and continue being awesome. As always, let me know if I can be of any help. Take care.

Samrat

■ ■ ■

WHEN I WROTE THIS EMAIL, there were many thoughts going through my mind and no singular theme. The first was a struggle I was having on how far I should go in advising people about their personal choices. In mid-March 2021, the world was perplexed by and enamored with the dramatic drop in COVID-19 cases in India. Hypotheses included the possibility of herd immunity by way of many Indians having been unknowingly infected over the past year, the presence of stronger immune systems in developing countries given that people are exposed to viruses all the time, and the potential of less-rich diets and lower obesity rates helping to reduce mor-

---

[40] In cricket, a duck is when a batter gets a score of zero. Think of it like striking out in baseball—but way, way worse.

[41] In cricket, getting a boundary is like hitting it out of the park in baseball.

tality. In India, politicians declared victory over the virus and began to export vaccines to the rest of the world despite less than 5 percent of India's population having been vaccinated.

I will admit I was convinced that something magical had occurred—after all, for the first dozen years after moving to the US, I hardly ever got sick, which I attributed to the strong immune system I had built growing up in India. But I was also a tad bit nervous, and it made me queasy as I watched thousands of people in a stadium, dancing together with no masks or any precautions being taken. If I had been talking to my relatives, I would have said in an email, "This is risky, and I don't want to see any of you dropping your guard." But it is often a dilemma for business leaders how far they should go in providing personal advice. If they express their opinions to their teams as they would to their own family, there is a line that is crossed. If a family member files a grievance against another, it gets resolved through tense negotiations. However, if a team member files an HR complaint against a leader for having gone too far in expressing their opinions (however valid), it could mean the beginning of the end for the leader. Hence, most leaders take the safe stance: offer perspective, suggest or hint, but never dictate.

A couple of weeks after I sent this email, India was walloped by the resurgence of the virus in ways no one expected. Overnight more than 20 percent of my team was out either because of illness or to care for affected family members. It made me wish I had been more direct in my message, but I cannot convince myself that that would have been the right move.

The other phenomenon I was reflecting on was well-intended moves that go wrong when implemented across the board without due consideration for local needs. During the pandemic, burnout and stress management became a big theme in professional organizations. Task forces were convened to arrive at ideas for reducing Zoom fatigue, ensuring people could take the appropriate breaks, and helping people make the right choices for themselves. The intent of these various initiatives was noble, and they produced good ideas.

The trouble arose when one-size-fits-all solutions started getting dictated across the organization. One such example would be "meeting-free Fridays." In theory, this is a wonderful idea to allow people to focus on their individual tasks, avoid distractions, and wrap up early for the week. However, the unintended consequence was that the remaining four days of the week became packed with meetings. Eventually, on Fridays people would say, "I know we are not supposed to have a meeting, but we have to be ready for Monday. Could we just connect for thirty minutes?" This in turn would blow up professional social networking sites like Fishbowl, where employees would complain, "I can't believe my manager doesn't know to respect my Fridays!"

My suggestion to task forces is to provide options to business folks rather than dictate strict rules. The larger the organization, the more the heterogeneity in situations, business context, and personal choice. Almost any blanket rule is likely to be met with fifty-fifty enthusiasm. It is smarter to encourage each person to work with their project teams to determine what works best for the group. In one team, the manager might prefer to take Friday afternoons off but is able to review deliverables from the team over the weekend and have feedback ready for them on Monday morning when they return. In another case, the entire team might prefer to wrap a neat bow around all deliverables, even if it requires a late Friday evening, as they prefer to not have anything hanging over them over the weekend and to ensure a relaxed start to the following week.

The last theme I was reflecting on in this email was my concern about the lack of respect we show others through our use of technology—without even realizing it. Admittedly, I am a byproduct of a generation where our first exposure to a computer was the IBM XT 286. Smartphones still befuddle me. (Every once in a while I find myself ranting inside my head, "How are these things not worse than cigarettes? Their whole design is intended to create the most addictive behavior possible for these young people who cannot take their eyes and hands off their darn phone." I'm sure in twenty-five years we'll be reviewing research on the mental effects these phones have created.) I take notes on a physical notepad, wear a tie to work every day, and never use text messages with my business colleagues.

However informal and cool people want to make the workplace, in our professional lives we still owe a degree of courtesy and respect to our colleagues. Random side banter via text messages or on chat or comment features only indicates that people are not focused on the topic at hand or don't care for the speaker. I will concede that not every speaker is good. But in the digital world, rather than start a firestorm of useless chat messages, perhaps the responsible thing to do is to disconnect from the call and come back when you think there is something of interest to you.

While the digital world provides many advantages in the way we connect and communicate with others, sometimes I have to remind myself to behave the same way as I would in an in-person meeting. If I were not interested in a speaker on stage, I would not start passing out notes to other participants or slump in my chair looking uninterested. Maybe it is the old-fashioned tie-wearing person in me, but a dose of good old mutual respect goes a long way in preserving relationships between speaker and listener.

Saturday, March 27, 2021

To: Compellium Team
From: Samrat Shenbaga
Subject: HAPPY HOLI FROM AMITABH BACHCHAN

Compellium Team:

Sorry for the clickbait but there is no personal message from Mr. Bachchan[42] here. ☹ When I realized that Monday is Holi,[43] I was reminded that Amitabh Bachchan has some of the best Holi songs in Indian movie history. (See https://youtu.be/Jf92MOkrbEw.[44]) Hence, I decided to watch one of my favorite Amitabh movies called *Hum* from 1991. To set the stage:

- No one will give this movie any editing awards as it is 3 hours long. I started on Thursday night and am still not done.

---

[42] Amitabh Bachchan is a mega-famous Indian actor.

[43] Holi is the Hindu festival of spring/love/colors, during which people throw colored powder on each other. It's more fun than it sounds.

[44] If any of these links gets broken by the time you read this book, use your finely honed googling skills to search YouTube for something similar.

- It stars the Indian movie industry equivalent of NBA legends Michael Jordan, Magic Johnson, and Larry Bird in the form of Amitabh Bachchan, Rajnikanth, and Govinda.
  - ☐ Bachchan is an easy one. There is no other movie star in the world who has captured the imagination of over 500 MM people for 5 decades running. (See famous scenes here: https://youtu.be/G2_IyucxIEo.)
  - ☐ If you fancy receiving a beatdown, I suggest saying "Rajni sucks" when in Chennai. Click on this link (https://youtu.be/6EdTiZ0jH8c) to understand why.
  - ☐ Some may debate my personal favorite, Govinda, as do people with Bird. I make my case based on the comparison of the original *Coolie No. 1* vs. the recent disastrous remake. (See comparison here: https://youtu.be/5cuRVwfMXEE.)
- *Hum* has the standard flaws of its time, most prominent of which is the lack of female casting. And it is the stereotypical Bollywood masala movie with fight scenes, impromptu dance sequences, and really random melodrama.

However, as I watched this movie, I was struck by valuable takeaways I should be applying in life. None of these occurred to the 15-year-old me when I first saw it on the big screen.

- **Use your star power (or bully pulpit) to spread important messages.** As I mentioned, this movie is lacking in gender diversity and is for the most part a run-of-the-mill entertainer. However, there is a scene where Bachchan steps in forcefully when a man is about to hit his wife and provides a blistering dialog against domestic violence. Later in the movie, a homemaker is overwhelmed with the demands of the various males in the household (husband, old guy, truant younger brother-in-law). The scene plays out in such a way that the men come to realize their follies and stop to appreciate/value the tremendous impact the lone woman in the household has. It was nice to see that even in a for-profit and often vain industry, the superstars recognized their responsibility to affect positive societal change. It serves as a good reminder for me that I should not lose sight of doing the right things even while in pursuit of revenue and profit.

- **Humility to evolve is important for long-term success**. From 1972–88, any Amitabh movie had only one hero—Amitabh. Then came a time in the late '80s where his star power went into decline. It was painful to see him doing dance routines with heroines two decades his junior. This phenomenon has been repeated countless times in Indian cinema where a superstar cannot reinvent themselves and eventually becomes unemployable. Bachchan is the exception: he had the smarts and humility to realize that he had to make way for the next generation while adapting his own roles. In this movie, he starts out as the young man, but very soon the storyline moves to where he is the elder gentleman. If you review Bachchan's career, over the most recent 30 years he has arguably done bigger and better things than he did in his first 20, which were thought of as his heyday. In professional careers too, it is important to realize that one has to continue to evolve, grow the next generation, and know when to get the hell out of the way.

- **People who get less of the limelight drive a disproportionate amount of the success.** Clearly the 3 stars brought in the crowds. But the supporting cast of Anupam Kher, Danny Denzongpa, and Kader Khan is what really makes the movie great. Their star power isn't nearly as high, but their talent is significantly better (sorry, Rajni fans—no Chennai for me). Something for us to keep in mind—flash and dazzle will get the attention of clients, but we always need to have exceptional substance to earn their respect.

If you have time to kill, the movie is on Amazon Prime. To all in India, wishing you a Happy Holi—with the virus situation it won't be as festive as always, but I hope there are ways to have a safe celebration. And to everyone, you continue to fill me with great Pride and Joy with all the amazing things you do. As always let me know if I can be of any help— and what you think of *Hum*!

Samrat

■ ■ ■

I WILL BE THE FIRST to admit that my unflinching fandom of Amitabh Bachchan colors how I think of his accomplishments, and I advise caution on the comparisons below. When I was young, my entire weekend would brighten when someone would say, "You kind of look like Amitabh Bachchan" (only to be surpassed by an incident when I was thirty-five and walking on Rodeo Drive in Beverly Hills and a young lady exclaimed to her friend, "Isn't that the guy from *Slumdog Millionaire*?"). However, I strongly believe that all business leaders should learn from the career of Bachchan, because many professional careers follow part or all of his arc in life.

When he started acting in the early 1970s, Bachchan took on niche roles behind the superstars of the day. His deep voice combined with his smooth style of acting kept raising his profile as he obtained increasingly bigger roles. The same is true for successful professionals. Early in their careers, they have to demonstrate expertise in an area. They will not be in the limelight as that is reserved for more senior members of the team. However, a strong performer starts separating from the pack and progresses quickly.

Once Mr. Bachchan became the main character in movies, he seemed to stumble upon an unmet need amongst the Indian population. Until that time, male Indian movie stars were portrayed as gentlemen—romantics and good "role models." However, the rising corruption in India was leading to an undercurrent of discontent in the populace. The "angry young man" broke through in stunning fashion when Bachchan took on roles where he would smash corrupt police officers and politicians. He smoked on screen, his drunken speeches to himself in the mirror are etched in Indian movie history, and he engaged in dance sequences that until then had been considered below a screen hero's dignity. Bollywood became a one-man industry for over a decade, and every one of Bachchan's movies drew record reception.

Successful business leaders have similar traits. Once they've distinguished themselves early in their careers through expertise, they look for areas that are underserved and present an opportunity. This could be starting a new business line that others are unwilling to take a risk on, spearheading a turnaround that most don't have the appetite for, or building a business in a location that requires personal sacrifices like moving one's family. But to be a business leader that stands out, one has to take risk. And it can't be a calculated risk—at some point one will have to take a leap of faith and hope for the best.

After tremendous success, Mr. Bachchan hit a nearly two-decade lull. There are many reasons that movie historians will cite, but in my mind he just got lazy. His movies were more of the same, and as he entered his mid-40s, he was upstaged by newcomers who adapted better to the needs of the audience. Bachchan jumped into politics because of his brand name and, after being mired in some shady deals, exited in disrepute within a few short months. Then he launched his own production house, again banking on his brand name. It went bankrupt.

The phenomenon of "treat me with respect for what I did yesterday as opposed to what I am doing today" is all too common in the corporate world. Leaders who have twenty-plus years of experience achieve titles and then suddenly almost stop trying. For a while, their stories of "when we were growing this firm, I used to run all the jobs" are met with awe and admiration. However, it doesn't take long before the younger team members start wondering what value the tenured leader actually brings. And before you know it a much more energetic person leaps ahead. Depending on the organization, the tenured leader is either tolerated but ignored or gradually shown the exit. "Getting lazy" is the death knell for a business leader.

Most Indians (myself included) assumed that Bachchan was done for. Then, in the early 2000s, something amazing happened. Bachchan became the host for the Indian equivalent of *Who Wants to Be a Millionaire?* Most viewed this move as an act of desperation, as it was widely considered a demotion for a movie star to move to television. And maybe it was desperation. But to everyone's surprise the show became one of the biggest hits in Indian TV history. Bachchan's presence on screen, quick wit, and booming voice made every episode a must-watch episode. Suddenly Bachchan's movie career saw a revival. Having learned his lesson, he took on roles where he was the senior citizen and co-starred with the top names of the day. His brand name shone bright again. And he didn't stop there. He experimented with singing, took on offbeat roles, and tried things that had never been done before (people were stunned when he danced to a rap song in one of his movies—something not even the younger generation had dared do). Now age seventy-eight, in Indian movies he is as big a name as it comes.

Business leaders too will be faced with adversity at some point in their career. The most common result is that they wilt and live their career out in a job that does not satisfy them but that pays the bills. The way to get back in the game is to double down on the risk. Perhaps that means stepping down to something "less prestigious" and relearning skills while partnering with more junior people. But an experienced business leader always has the benefit of hindsight and the ability to learn from their mistakes. And if they can be fearless in the new reality that faces them, success is guaranteed.

CONCLUSION

(What I Learned)

■ ■ ■

WE ALL KNOW when the pandemic started. It is less certain when it will end, especially as we look across the globe and at those far less fortunate than the United States. But there is hope and optimism for the world. As for myself, I feel I come out of the pandemic a different and presumably better person than when I went into it. Perhaps many of the changes I sense would have occurred anyway with my mid-forties creeping up on me, but there is no denying that the pandemic has been a statistically significant inflection point.

The first change I feel is a sensation of calmness, or perhaps an increased maturity. The pandemic slowed down the passage of time in front of my eyes. As a result, I saw, experienced, and thought of things that I'd never taken time for before. Life came into perspective. While I was fortunate not to be afflicted by the virus, many others I knew were not so lucky. And some, sadly, passed away. The early death of someone you know is the ultimate reset button to your own selfish drive for power and money. Prior to the pandemic, I would be annoyed by the smallest of issues. If the government raised taxes by 2 percent, I was mad. If I didn't get praised for winning a big deal, I felt disrespected. Now when encountering such negative feelings, I remind myself that I'm alive and that even if I never worked another day in my life, I'd be okay (not Warren Buffet-okay but still okay). I suppose the key here is that if pessimists are self-aware, then they can train themselves to move towards becoming realists. (And who knows—maybe someday optimists.)

The second change I experienced was the realization that I should not be swayed by one viewpoint or the other. It is best to listen to various perspectives, understand where those perspectives are coming from, research the facts, and come to one's own conclusions. The only thing I found more distressing than the pandemic itself was the rising decibel levels on television with each news entity promoting a certain narrative. It was as if Sean Hannity and Chris Cuomo were living in alternate universes. Initially the constant hypocrisy, occasional stupidity, and incessant sanctimony got under my skin. But as time went by, I realized that they each had a job to do and business objectives to meet even if it meant sensationalizing the events of the day. They are surrounded by people who hold the same beliefs, they look for data to confirm their convictions, and they view the other side as an existential threat. Hence, I decided to search for my own facts. We live in a wonderful world where we are only a Google search away from finding almost any information we might need or want. As I mentioned earlier, Worldometer became my bible for tracking the pandemic. It clearly presented trends in infections and deaths by country and state. I could look at the data points and decide for myself whether I should feel hopeful, or double up on the masks. As vaccinations rolled out, I became a religious follower of the daily updates from the Florida Department of Health to understand the uptake curves and calculate when my turn would arrive. And as I learned about the seasonal variations in data, saw clear trends, and found my own prediction accuracy improving, I was able to discount the loud opinions all around me. Not that I was right all the time, but at least I felt more in control.

The most important realization I had during the pandemic was the power of teams. Even though we were physically separated, the bonds grew stronger on our global team. During Zoom calls, people got to peek into each other's living rooms, learn to recognize dog barks, see babies. My personal communications to the team served as a relief mechanism by which I could communicate how I was feeling. These emails became a bit of an obsession that kept my mind off darker things. And I could not be happier to be part of a team that cares for each other and looks to lift each other up.

As consultants, we are trained to develop an executive summary for every presentation. If I were to distill the forty-five thousand words in this book, I would offer these ten takeaways:

1. No communication is perfect, but you can't go wrong when it's heartfelt.
2. Understanding individual motivations is critical to shaping the right experience for the team.
3. Constant reinvention is the key to a successful and satisfactory career.
4. When the team is ready, a good leader gets out of the way.
5. Tell the team the truth—they can handle it.
6. Set the right conditions, and then let people make their own choices.
7. Occasionally saying "I don't know" adds credibility to an expert.
8. Apply to yourself what you believe is good for others.
9. Have a vision for the future, but don't get obsessed with it.
10. Listen to all sides and then make the best call possible.

I have found that there is no science to being a business leader, a participant in society, or a simple family man. I tell my teams that my favorite president is George W. Bush, not necessarily for every decision that he made but for the fact that he was a man of conviction. He realized that one can debate till one goes blue in the face about the merits and downsides of any decision. But periodically a tough call has to be made and a leader must rely on their gut; if their motivations are pure and they are aware of their own biases, there is a better than fifty-fifty chance they come out ahead. (And, hey, if it doesn't work out, then there is the famous Bushism: "I'll be long gone before some smart person ever figures out what happened inside this Oval Office.")

On balance, the pandemic brightened my outlook on humankind and my ability to be a positive contributor. I certainly hope there can be an infusion of optimism across the board so that we can all build empathy, respect, and compassion for one another. And if the cacophony of the media or politicians gets to be too much, I have found an easy solution that has existed for a long time and is even more powerful now—the venerable remote control. It has on/off and channel-changing buttons. Best of all it takes me to the vast world of streaming, where I can watch old episodes of *Seinfeld* and YouTube videos of Conan O'Brien commencement speeches.

And that makes me happy.

EPILOGUE

Monday, August 16, 2021

To: Compellium Team
From: Samrat Shenbaga
Subject: WORDS OF ADVICE
FROM RILEY THE DOG

Compellium Team:

2021 is moving fast and we continue to adapt to the various changes the pandemic throws at us. Through it all, this team outdoes itself in scaling newer and higher peaks. I feel great pride and joy to be part of a team that is driving tremendous client impact, maintaining compassion and camaraderie, and constantly innovating. Well done and let's keep doing more of it.

Last year around this time, I mentioned to you that August 15th holds special significance for me. As most know, it is India's Independence Day. This August 15th was my 25th anniversary of arriving in America. Coincidentally, it also marked the 10th anniversary of the San Diego office opening which I was a proud part of. It was also to be Riley's 9th birthday—however, he fell slightly short when he passed away peacefully on Thursday, August 12th. I say "however" instead of "sadly" or "unfortunately" because he lived a very full life and went out just the way he would want—in the tranquility and comfort of his own backyard. Riley's life had an odd symmetry to it—the first night he came home as a puppy I slept next to him on the floor and I did the same thing on his last night. And on both occasions it was to help him get out to the yard to use the facilities.

Dogs are the best educators and I learnt a lot from him over the course of 9 years. So in honor of Riley, I share the **top 3 Rileyisms** and how they apply to us:

- *If one wants to go in the pool, then they just must.* To describe Riley as "stubborn" would be the understatement of the year. His singular focus in life was to get in the pool, but then he'd get bad ear infections from the water. I tried a number of contraptions and pool fences to keep him out, but to no avail. He would patiently find a way to break through. In the attached picture, he managed to rip the screen from the patio entrance after 10 days of persistent head butting just so he could head to the pool when no one was looking. In our professional careers, there are a multitude of opportunities in front of us. The Compellium account provides a ton of variety, the firm has multiple options, and the world is full of possibilities. So if we want to explore new areas, we should go get them. As the Compellium team and the firm continue to grow, I would encourage each one of us to chase what we are passionate about (just don't break the rules as much as Riley did!).

- *Leave a lot of hair on people's clothes and they will love you forever.* Riley was prone to greet anyone and everyone with gusto regardless of whether it had been 5 minutes since he saw them last or 5 years (or never before). He also had a coat of hair that shed like no one's business. So everyone was assured a good dose of Riley hair when they left our home. It came as no surprise that I got notes from people in 7 states and 3 countries offering their sympathies—I am sure there is Riley hair in all those places! Over the years, I have been asked what our firm's secret sauce is—and the answer is always that "it's our people." Our firm's DNA is one of having empathy for the needs of clients and colleagues. Our people will go above and beyond to ensure their clients are successful. And as a result clients love us forever and want to keep working with us. So keep spilling your secret sauce on clients and colleagues and you'll be loved forever.

- *To be cool you must be crazy.* We always described Riley as someone with the best heart but with lots of screws loose in the head. He always insisted on being in my home office. And just when I needed to speak on a Zoom call, he would roll on his back and make the wildest noises. Many a time I apologized to clients and teammates that it was not a case of me snoring or grunting at what they were saying—it was just Riley. But that wild behavior kept things exciting. Riley would want all of us to be a bit crazy and do something that we wanted to do, even if it were frowned upon. Let's push the boundaries on everything we touch.

If each of us injects ourselves with some **Rileyism**, it will be a wild ride! Thank you for everything you do for each other and for our clients. Let me know if I can be of any help or assistance.

Samrat

Figure 17. Riley coming through the screen door (literally)

Figure 18. Riley's wild happiness

Figure 19. Riley the swimmer

■ ■ ■

MY BEST GUESS is that each of the emails in this book initially took me two to four hours to create. That estimate includes the time to think of content, create an initial draft, kick the tires to ensure I was being mildly humorous but not insensitive, and then pushing it out. My notes on my iPhone are full of reminders I wrote to myself while on the golf course about things I could point out. For this particular email, I spent an additional two to four hours deliberating whether to send it out at all and, if I did, what the right timing would be. I didn't want team members getting despondent. And with the team spanning multiple time zones, it was a delicate balance. For sure I didn't want to ruin people's weekend by sending a sad story on a Sunday. But even sending it during the day on Monday could mean that some people would read it first thing in their time zone.

Eventually I decided that it was the right thing for me to share and pushed the send button at 10 a.m. on Monday. Many on the team had shared their personal struggles and setbacks during the pandemic. It would be unfair for me not to fully share my own life. I believe a good leader must display vulnerability as much as they portray strength. It is important for teams to realize their leaders are human too and not stoic strategists. After all, as a team we spend nine of our seventeen waking hours together five days a week—it's best that we lean on one another.

The heartfelt responses to this email drummed up even more emotions than when I called the vet's office to let them know that Riley had made his decision to go. I will forever be indebted to my Compellium team for their warmth and caring. And I cannot thank Riley enough for being by my side during my journey as a leader, a father, and a human being.

ACKNOWLEDGEMENTS

THANKS TO MY mother-in-law, Donna Zicha, who was the fastest early reader to get through the manuscript and displayed immense enthusiasm for it. Thanks to my wife, Margo, and daughter, Siena, for their constructive feedback and encouragement. While my father provided the most detailed advice, I have reserved his extensive thoughts for my next book. Liz Torp gave me invaluable insights on viewing the book through the lens of others. Many beta readers deserve credit for bravely navigating the 45,000 words and giving me healthy pointers. Mazen Zahlan has been a good friend who provided support and candid feedback. Rajat Jain gave me his usual balanced and sage advice. Nick Shaw is a trusted advisor and summarized the takeaways from this book like only he can. I thank Chris Wright for reading the manuscript and giving it an enthusiastic thumbs up and more importantly for being a leader that I enjoyed growing up under—he will never know the incredible impact he has had on me personally and professionally.

This book would not be a reality if not for Karin Wiberg of Clear Sight Books. Her counsel, enthusiasm, and clear direction moved a collection of my notes to an actual book. I will be forever indebted to her for earning me the title of Author. If anyone has an idea for a book but doesn't know how to turn it into reality, I recommend they talk to Karin.

AUTHOR BIO

SAMRAT SHENBAGA is a management consultant who has worked with global corporations on a variety of issues for the past twenty-five years. He loves the many facets of his job, with his favorite part being the opportunity to work with team members across the globe; they teach him something new every day and constantly inspire him. Samrat believes that life and work are interconnected, and he strives to apply lessons from one to the other, including connecting the dots between his experiences growing up in India and his adult life in the US.

Printed in the USA
CPSIA information can be obtained
at www.ICGtesting.com
LVHW091453101123
763181LV00110B/217/J